GOD
Thought of Everything
WEiRD
and WACKY

Written by Bonnie Bruno

Illustrated by Kevin Brown

Standard
PUBLISHING
CINCINNATI, OHIO

Dedication

To Caleigh, whose love for critters sparked the idea for this book.

Project editor: Greg Holder
Jacket design: Tobias' Outerwear for Books
Interior design: Tobias' Outerwear for Books

Scripture taken from the HOLY BIBLE, NEW INTERNATIONAL READER'S VERSION™. Copyright © 1995, 1996, 1998 by International Bible Society. Used by permission of Zondervan Publishing House. All rights reserved.
ISBN 0-7847-1447-9

09 08 07 06 05 04 03   9 8 7 6 5 4 3 2 1

TABLE OF CONTENTS

God Thought of Everything Weird and Wacky

Psssssst! Wanna Know a Secret?

If you have access to the Internet, here's a website especially for you. All 60 links mentioned in this book are available at a special website created by the author. This will save you the headache of having to type every single URL in your browser. Just click on a link and go!

To access the *God Thought of Everything Weird and Wacky* links page, type the following URL in your browser window:

http://www.bonniebruno.com/godthought1.htm

WHEN TROUBLE HITS, I CLICK 'N FLIP

God created me with a hard shell and six legs. He gave me joints similar to the joints you have in your knees and elbows. I need joints to bend my six legs so I can safely crawl along branches. I also need claws at the end of each leg. Without claws, I would not be able to cling to branches and leaves, or crawl through wet and slippery grass.

God knew there would be times when I would slip and fall. He knew that I would need a way to pick myself up again. So he gave me a special spine on the bottom of my middle section. The spine fits into a little groove on my underbelly. If I accidentally fall and land upside-down, I just arch my body like an athlete and flip right-side up again with a quick *CLICK*! How clever is *that*?

And if a hungry critter wanders into my territory, my set of antennae picks up his sound and movement. I tuck my antennae and legs close to my body and lie very still. My enemy thinks I'm dead, and loses interest fast! I can do this for hours if I need to, until danger passes.

God thought of everything when he created me—**Click Beetle.**

More on the Web

You have a family name, don't you? So do I! I come from the *elateridae* family of beetles. Here is a picture of one of my colorful cousins from Costa Rica:

http://nathist.sdstate.edu/SMIRCOL/Costa_Rica/Elaters/main.htm

Tell a Friend

Everybody has problems now and then. Problems don't have to flip us around, though! God is our helper, and promises to be there for us always.

Read About It

"I trust in God. I praise his word. I trust in God. I will not be afraid. What can people do to me?"—Psalm 56:4

One of my cousins has two false eyes— big round spots on its head that scare away predators.

Pray About It

Thanks, God, for watching over me night and day.

WHAT'S FOR DINNER?

I'm a hungry plant that grows only in wet areas, like waterlogged meadows or bogs. If you visit me in the springtime, I'll wow you with my purple petals and yellow *sepals* (these are small leaves that cup the bottom of a flower). The rest of the year, though, I'm just a bundle of tightly packed leaves. I look like a giant green apostrophe attached to a thick, greenish-yellow stalk. My speckly purple or reddish top stands out from the surrounding plants and I usually grow to a height of 10 to 20 inches.

My stalk looks harmless enough, but if you are an insect, watch out! Under my colorful curved hood lies a hidden passageway—a secret opening into my stalk. Like a dainty dessert, my stalk is lined with sweet nectar, luring buggy types inside for a taste. Once I capture them, I invite them to wander deeper into my hollow tube, where they can try to escape. I trick the insects with fake areas that appear to be exits. But these areas really lead deeper into my deadly stalk.

Thick clumps of downward-pointing hairs prevent the insects from returning to the top of the stalk.

At the bottom lies a pool of water—and no escape. The water is filled with bacteria that liquify the insects, turning them into nitrogen. That makes them easy to digest. *Yum*! Dinner has never tasted so good!

God thought of everything when he created me—**Cobra Lily.**

More on the Web

Want to see three special panoramas of my home at Darlingtonia State Natural Site in Oregon?

http://www.oregonstateparks.org/park_115.php?md=pic

Tell a Friend

The cobra lily tricks visitors to step inside, then entraps them. Temptation is like that, too, but God is always there to help when we call on him.

Read About It

"He himself suffered when he was tempted. Now he is able to help others who are being tempted."—Hebrews 2:18

My real name is Darlingtonia Californica, but people call me cobra lily because my hood reminds them of a cobra snake. I live mostly on the west coast of the United States, in California and Oregon.

Pray About It

Lord, thank you for being there to help me turn my back on temptation.

A FACE ONLY A MOM COULD LOVE

I f you could request your favorite foods all in one meal, what would you eat? I would order fish, fish, and more fish!

I'm a member of the bat family, with the official name of *noctilio leporinus.* Members of my species live mostly in Central and South America. I'm known for my unusual face, which is shaped like a bulldog.

Who needs a fishing pole with equipment like mine? I make chirping noises, which bounce off the surface of the water. That helps me locate the ripples left behind by fish. I can even detect how deep they are swimming.

I then swoop down with my oversized hind feet and large, hooked claws. I know how to spear a fish with sharp canine teeth, then crush its skull. God made my cheeks out of stretchy membrane, with special pouches as storage space for hauling fish home to my roost in hollowed-out trees or abandoned buildings. Sometimes I devour my fish in the air as I fly. I can eat 30 to 40 fish each night!

You might have seen me following pelicans around in the late afternoon as they skim the water for fish. I let the pelicans fish first, and plunge in after whatever they miss. Sneaky, don't you think?

If I'm craving a quick snack away from the water, I'll settle for crickets, beetles, winged ants, and stinkbugs—but oh, how I love those fish!

God thought of everything when he created me—**Bulldog Fishing Bat.**

More on the Web

Here's a picture of me resting between fishing trips.

http://animaldiversity.ummz.umich.edu/media/phil/noctilio_leporinus_2.jpg

Tell a Friend

God supplies all of his creation with food as they need it. He also supplies his people with spiritual food from his Word. How does the Bible satisfy your spiritual appetite?

Read About It

"Blessed are those who are hungry and thirsty for what is right. They will be filled."—Matthew 5:6

In the Leviticus chapter 11 God instructs the Israelites not to eat certain animals and insects. He called them "unclean." Bats are mentioned in verse 19.

Pray About It

Dear God, help me to hunger after your Word just like I crave my favorite foods.

FRIENDS CALL ME "DIGGER"

God planned for females of my species to have four babies at a time—every time they give birth!

My big family originally came from Mexico. Over the years, my aunts, uncles, and cousins spread throughout the southeastern United States. Other relatives live in South America. In fact, there are over 20 different types of our species in the world. Imagine what a family reunion would look like!

God knew that I would need tools for digging, so he equipped me with long, powerful claws. I use them like shovels to dig a cozy burrow underground. There I spend my days, tucked away from predators. When night falls, I leave my home to forage for food.

I crave ants and termites the way you love pizza and hamburgers. Using my shovel feet, I tunnel into a termite's nest. Once I create that passageway, I lean in close and stick my snout into the hole. My long, sticky tongue lashes out and grabs a mouthful of wriggling goodies. *Yum!*

God gave me a special coat of armor to protect me from predators. The armor is made of bands of hard, bony plates. Between each band lies a flexible layer of skin, which allows me to move my legs. This special suit protects my head, shoulders, hips, and tail. To protect my soft belly, I pull in my legs and press my underside hard against the ground. Sometimes I pull my feet in and roll up in a tight ball, too.

God thought of everything when he created me—**Armadillo.**

More on the Web

An armadillo's teeth are not protected by enamel like the teeth of other mammals. Find out why at Armadillo Online:

http://www.msu.edu/~nixonjos/armadillo/

Tell a Friend

God provides for an armadillo's daily needs. In what ways does God provide for you and your family?

Read About It

"Give thanks no matter what happens. God wants you to thank him because you believe in Christ Jesus."—1 Thessalonians 5:18

My eyes are very sensitive to light. I only come out during cloudy weather, late afternoon, or at night.

Pray About It

Dear God, thank you for creating me and taking care of me.

MORE THAN A SHADE TREE

I've been called the tree that God planted upside-down. My thick trunk ends in a wild tangle of root-like branches at the top. They look like skinny arms waving at the sky. I originated in Africa, and because of the enormous size of my trunk, experts believe that I am thousands of years old. It is hard to estimate my exact age, though, because my trunk does not have any rings to count.

If the world held a contest to find the most useful tree, I might win. My leaves are cooked as a vegetable similar to spinach. They are also used to treat insect bites, and other medical conditions like asthma and kidney problems. I blossom when I am about 20 years old. Pollen from my flowers is mixed with water to make glue.

God made me useful to travelers. My flowers wilt within 24 hours and fall to the ground, where their petals are eaten by birds. My vitamin-rich fruits and seeds provide food for a weary passerby. Hollow out my huge trunk, and you can sleep inside me. In some places, my trunk is even used as a water storage tank.

If you like music, use the fiber of my bark to make a stringed instrument. It can also be used to make rope, cloth, and baskets. I'll grow new bark wherever the old bark is stripped away.

God thought of everything when he created me—**Baobab Tree.**

More on the Web

Here's a gigantic baobab tree in Barbados, said to have been transported there from Africa in 1738!

http://www.barbados.org/baobab.htm

Tell a Friend

The baobab tree is a giver. In the same way, God is honored when we help those in need.

Read About It

"Anyone who is kind to poor people lends to the Lord. God will reward him for what he has done."—Proverbs 19:17

My flowers give off a musky scent, and bloom only at night. The moonlit blossoms attract fruit bats, which drink the nectar and pass my pollen from flower to flower.

Pray About It

Lord, you have given me gifts to share with others. Help me to honor you through my actions and thoughts.

A PESKY PICNIC PARTY POOPER

Nobody invites me to a family campout or backyard barbecue. I spend most of my life dodging people who chase me down and swat at me. I beat my wings 165 to 200 times per second—over twice the speed of a hummingbird! Special muscles work to lift and lower my wings. A small opening in my midsection pulls in air when I flap my wings. That's how God supplies oxygen to my tiny muscles, because I don't have lungs like humans.

I am attracted to strong smells, like sweet flowers, rotting fruit, or a nice fresh pile of pig or cow manure. I don't have teeth for chewing, so a drop or two of vomit helps dissolve food into a liquid treat. I can also peel my lips back if necessary, and use the sharp, jagged edge of my mouth for scraping food in hard-to-reach places. You have taste buds on your tongue, but mine are in and around my mouth, and even on my *feet*. That's right—I can taste with my tootsies!

So, hold onto your hamburgers! Protect your hotdogs! I'm always on the lookout for my next meal, and trust me—you do not want me to land anywhere near your plate. I may not be welcome at your next family reunion, but I do have a purpose in life: I provide a scrumptious snack for snakes and frogs!

God thought of everything when he created me—**Housefly.**

More on the Web

Watch assorted insects in action! These movie clips include a fly nibbling on a piece of bread.

http://www.cinenet.com/footage/samples/bugs/page4.html

Tell a Friend

God has a purpose for every living thing. He created you with a special plan in mind—a plan that will use your unique talents and abilities.

Read About It

"God is working in you. He wants your plans and your acts to be in keeping with his good purpose."
—Philippians 2:13

Pray About It

Lord, I want to know your special plan for my life. Help me to walk close to you as I discover it.

I have wraparound eyes that help me sense movement nearby. My eyes work ten times faster than a human eye.

THE STINKY FLYING COW

I'm a happy *folivore*—a bird who thrives on leaves. Most birds dream of their next plump meal of insects, seeds, or fruits, but if I had to choose a special birthday dinner, I'd request a pile of chewy leaves. For dessert, I'd nibble sweet berries.

I began life without feathers, in a messy nest overlooking the flooded plains of central Venezuela. When monkeys or snakes came near, I would dive into the waters below. There I learned to swim well, long before I could fly. God equipped me with two front claws, so that when the coast was clear, I could run back up the tree trunk to the safety of my nest again. He planned for the claws to fall off once I learned to fly.

I'm fully grown now, with chestnut-brown feathers framing a bright blue face and red eyes. A strip of colorful feathers sits atop my head like a fancy hat. Sometimes I am mistaken for a pheasant, but my closest relative is the cuckoo. I am the size of a plump chicken, and I smell like cow manure. Onlookers often make fun of my clumsy movements. I've been called names like "flying cow" or even worse— "stinkbird."

Because leaves are tough to digest, I store ground-up leaves in a pouch in my throat called a *crop*. There they soak in bacteria to soften and prepare it for digestion—much the way a cow digests grass.

God thought of everything when he created me—**Hoatzin.**

More on the Web

Take a photo tour of the hoatzin's habitat in the Amazon jungle!

http://www.junglephotos.com/animals/birds/hoatzin.html

Tell a Friend

The hoatzin is one of the oddest birds alive, and has earned a strange reputation for itself. The Bible cautions us about labeling people who look different. Remember that God looks at the heart, not at how we look.

Read About It

"I do not look at the things people look at. Man looks at how someone appears on the outside. But I look at what is in the heart."

—1 Samuel 16:7

I was described in science books for the first time in 1775.

Pray About It

Heavenly Father, help me to see others the way you do—from the inside out.

HOMEBODY AT HEART

The desert is the only place I have ever known. My burrow home is shaped like an upside-down "U," and is only three inches in diameter. At the bottom of the "U" is a cool, flat area where I rest. I only wander out at night, when the temperatures are cooler.

I measure 10 inches from head to tail, but my bushy tail is longer than my body. God knew I would need to spring across the loose, soft sand of my home in the southwestern United States. He designed my large, hairy-soled back feet bigger than my two front feet. I have four toes on each hind foot, while many of my cousins have five. My shorter front feet have strong claws, which are perfect for digging my deep burrow.

I have long puzzled scientists for several reasons. For one thing, I don't sweat or pant to keep my body cool, like other animals. Water is scarce here in the desert, but guess what? My body changes dry seeds into liquid nourishment! Kidneys usually need lots of water to rid the body of waste, but my Maker gave me special kidneys. They work just fine without water. I'm not like a camel, which stores water in its body for future use. I don't store a single drop of water, and yet, experiments have shown that my body has as much water content as other animals!

God thought of everything when he created me—**Kangaroo Rat.**

More on the Web

Meet my cousin, the Texas kangaroo rat:

http://www.tpwd.state.tx.us/adv/kidspage/animals/k-rat.htm

Tell a Friend

The kangaroo rat does not venture too far from home. He has found contentment in familiar surroundings. What does *home* mean to you?

Read About It

"You gain a lot when you live a godly life. But you must be happy with what you have. We didn't bring anything into the world. We can't take anything out of it. If we have food and clothing, we will be happy with that."—1 Timothy 6:6-8

Pray About It

Lord, I am grateful that you take care of all my needs. Thank you for preparing an eternal home in heaven that will be mine someday.

If a rattlesnake slithers near, I turn and kick sand into its face.

I LOVE A GOOD HUG!

I'll never win a trophy for having a friendly personality. Some even call me the bully of the jungle. But can I help that I'm hungry all the time?

My appetite has grown tremendously since my baby days, when I measured a wee 24 inches. At 22 feet long and 550 pounds, it takes a lot to satisfy me now! I'd much rather feast on a deer than a mouse, but I'll eat whatever is available if I'm hungry. Watch out, turtles! Watch out, iguanas! You're listed on my menu, too.

I have eyes on top of my head, which keep me alert for my next meal. When a tasty treat wanders my way, I don't mess around. I coil my powerful body around my victim and give it a gigantic hug until it quits breathing. God created me with a special jaw that unhinges. It allows me to open my mouth w-i-d-e and eat animals that would normally be too large to swallow.

On a sunny day, I'll sometimes slither to the water's edge and rest in the grass awhile. I wish God had not made me taste so good, though. Bloodsucking ticks find me whenever I settle down for a riverside nap. They march across my yellow and black back like soldiers in a parade. Ouch!

God thought of everything when he made me—**Anaconda**.

More on the Web
Visit me at the Nashville Zoo online:

http://www.nashvillezoo.org/anaconda.htm

Tell a Friend
God created each anaconda to be unique. How are you and your best friend different? In what ways are you alike?

Read About It
"God said, 'Let the land produce all kinds of living creatures. Let there be livestock, and creatures that move along the ground, and wild animals. Let there be all kinds of them.' And that's exactly what happened." —Genesis 1:24

I don't lay eggs; instead, I give birth to up to 100 wriggling, slithering babies at a time. Each of my babies has a different marking on the underside of its tail, just as humans have a different fingerprint.

Pray About It
Thanks for fitting the world together with so many unique parts, Lord!

READY...SET...FIRE AWAY!

Have you ever visited Java? Java is an island in Indonesia. Its mountains are home to my family and me. If you see a furry little creature with a beautiful white stripe running the length of its back, that's me! I may not be very big, but don't let my short, stocky appearance fool you. God equipped me with a smart way to protect myself from pushy predators. If an enemy startles or threatens my safety, I can make my body go completely limp and play dead. How's that for a slick trick? Or, depending on my mood, I can turn around, lift my short furry tail, and spray a toxic, oily green substance. I'm one of the best shots around, and can score a direct hit from over three feet away.

I sometimes don't notice when an enemy lurks nearby. The Javan hawk-eagle, for example, would love to swoop down and snatch me up for a tasty lunch. If I sense him circling overhead, I don't waste time figuring out what to do. I just trot off in the opposite direction to hide until he's gone.

Chances are slim that you'll ever bump into me. I only come out at night. Daylight hours find me resting inside my burrow. I dig my burrow with my sharp claws. At the bottom lies a roomy chamber, big enough for a bed. I make my bed from leaves, twigs, and other plant litter. My friend the porcupine likes my burrow so much, he sometimes curls up for a nap with me. He respects my stinky weapon, and I respect his prickly needles. Humans call ours an unusual friendship.

God thought of everything when he created me—**Stink Badger.**

More on the Web

How many other types of badgers do you think there are? Learn all about my widespread family at:

http://www.badgers.org.uk/badgerpages/stink-badgers-01.html

Tell a Friend

God taught the stink badger how to handle its enemies. Have you ever felt cornered by someone who treated you unkindly? Read today's verse and write it in your own words.

Read About It

"Instead, worship me. I will save you from the powerful hand of all your enemies." —2 Kings 17:39

I'm a Bible star! Psalm 104:18 speaks of the animals that live on cliffs, including badgers.

Pray About It

You have the answer to every problem, Lord. Thank you for loving and watching over me!

KING OF THE HOPPERS

If you think all frogs look the same, think again. God designed me different from all the others. My body measures over one foot across. I am bigger than a piece of toast, bigger than your hand, and way bigger than most books about frogs. Stretch my legs out straight, and I measure almost three feet long from nose to toe!

I live in sparkling mountain streams in Cameroon, a country located in west central Africa. Other members of my family live in swift-moving rivers that wind through the dense rain forest of Cameroon and Equatorial Guinea. I am a shy frog, plus you won't catch me croaking on warm summer nights, because I was born without a voice sac.

I don't have a voice, but I do have a gigantic hop! If you were to enter me in a frog jumping contest, guess who would win?

Scientists are puzzled by my size. For one thing, my mother's eggs are the same size as any other frog's eggs. And I was never bigger than the other tadpoles. Hmmmm . . . God must have planned for me to be a giant among my species! Who am I, to argue with my Creator?

God thought of everything when he created me—**Goliath Frog.**

More on the Web

How much bigger am I than the average backyard frog? Judge for yourself in this photo of me lying next to a fawn:

http://inky.50megs.com/pictures/giant.gif

Tell a Friend

The Bible refers to God as our potter. Every member of creation is a one-of-a-kind handiwork. God takes delight in his work. Have you thanked him lately for making you just as you are?

Read About It

"Lord, you are our Father. We are the clay. You are the potter. Your hands made all of us."—Isaiah 64:8

Pray About It

Lord, your world is filled with unusual creatures. I am unusual too—in a good way! Thank you for making me one-of-a-kind.

Another Goliath is mentioned in the Bible, but he isn't a frog. Read all about this gigantic man in 1 Samuel 17.

BRAINY AND BRAWNY—
THAT'S ME!

I was hatched inside a rocky den, six weeks after my mother hung a clump of eggs there. She watched over me while I developed inside the egg, squirting my shell with water and guarding it against predators. My family has over 150 species. Some grow only as big as a jellybean. The biggest weighs over 550 pounds, and measures almost 23 feet across!

I've been called the most mysterious and smartest creature in the ocean. God gave me an amazing brain and eight busy arms, called *tentacles*. Researchers have spent years studying my movements and habits, trying to understand why I'm so smart. Scientists know that my brain controls vision and movement. For example, if my next meal swims by, my brain jumps into high gear. It tells my arms which direction to target, and how fast to move.

Researchers also now believe that each of my eight arms know what the other is doing—just as your left hand knows what your right hand is up to. They hope to use the results of their research to create a robotic arm that will help people who have lost an arm in an accident. The arm would be designed much the way my tentacles are, with nerve centers that move when their brain tells it to. Can you blame me for bragging about being chosen for this special project?

God thought of everything when he created me—**Octopus.**

More on the Web

How well do you know an octopus? Here's a fun website adventure where you'll learn some cool facts about my family.

http://projects.edtech.sandi.net/encanto/octopus/research.htm#moreresearch

Tell a Friend

God made each of us brainy in a different way. He gave us abilities and talents to use for good. Think of a time when you felt big-headed and acted like a braggart. How did others react to that?

Read About It

"If you really want to become wise, you must begin by having respect for the Lord. To know the Holy One is to gain understanding."
—Proverbs 9:10

Pray About It

Dear Lord, thank you for loving me so. Give me a heart of wisdom, so I can please you in all I do.

My mother lays more than 100,000 eggs!

AN UNLIKELY FRIENDSHIP

Who ever heard of a friendship between ants and butterflies? Well, I have! I belong to a family of butterflies who depend on red ants for survival. God planned for us to become friends who cooperate.

During my caterpillar stage, I sent a signal to red ants, telling them it was time for them to adopt me. An ant showed up within minutes, and began tapping my body with its antennae. Ordinary ants would have eaten me for lunch, but not the red ant! It waited for me to release a droplet of sweet, honey-like nectar from my special nectary organ. The nectar is an important part of the ant's diet.

After the ant had eaten its fill, I flattened my body to make it easy for it to carry me to its nest. There it placed me in a special room where the ant larvae live. Worker ants treated me just like one of the family. They fed me so well, my body weight increased 100 times in one month!

I stayed with the ants throughout the fall, winter, and spring months, changing from caterpillar to pupa inside my cocoon. After hatching, I had to work my way through that ant-filled nest to an exit. Some ants didn't want me to leave, though! God protected me by covering my body with a hair-like armor of loose scales. When an ant tried to bite me, all it got was a mouthful of scales.

God thought of everything when he created me—**Alcon Blue Butterfly**.

More on the Web

Want to see red ants at work?

http://www.microscopy-uk.org.uk/mag/artmar01/dyoung5.html

Tell a Friend

God creates friendships when we least expect them. He uses creatures like ants and butterflies to teach us how to get along with one another. How did you and your best friend meet? Share why your friendship is so special.

Read About It

"Carry each other's heavy loads. If you do, you will give the law of Christ full meaning."—Galatians 6:2

Pray About It

Lord, thank you for giving me faithful friends who care about me.

In my caterpillar form, I will die unless I am adopted into a nest of ants.

HUMONGOUSLY HUNGRY

Have you noticed a small mouse-like critter scampering around your backyard or garden? Probably not, since I usually only come out at night. I live in a burrow underground, or beneath a pile of leaves or bark. Sometimes I even borrow a bedroom in the tunnel of a mouse or mole.

Members of my species vary in size from two to six inches, but don't let our small bodies fool you. Our appetites are humongous! God gave us the fastest metabolic rate of any animal. Every body function, from digestion to breathing, is speedy. For example, my heart beats 700 times a minute, and I breathe 10 times more often than you do!

Tiny mammals like me need lots of energy just to stay warm. I get my energy from eating, so I am forever on the lookout for food. I snack all day long on earthworms, berries, snails, and spiders. If I'm desperate, I'll sneak food from your pet's dish, too. I eat up to twice my body weight in food every single day!

My vision is not the best, but I have a keen sense of hearing, smell, and touch. My small size doesn't discourage me from making a meal of animals twice my size, either. How does a little guy like me protect himself? *Easy!* I smell like rotting garlic, so hungry animals don't venture too close.

God thought of everything when he created me—**Shrew**.

More on the Web

Read how a family from the Netherlands discovered a hungry shrew in their garden. Great photos, too!

http://www.gardensafari.net/first/shrews.htm

Tell a Friend

God gave the shrew a gigantic appetite for food. God's Word is often referred to as "food." When we take time to read the Bible, it makes us hungry for more.

Read About It

"Your words are very sweet to my taste! They are sweeter than honey to me."—Psalm 119:103

A 100 pound person would have to eat 200 pounds of food a day to keep up with my appetite.

Pray About It

Lord, I want to know you better. Give me a hunger to learn more about you.

GUESS WHAT'S ON THE MENU?

At first glance, you might think I'm just a filthy, good-for-nothing insect. After all, I survive by feeding on the dung from large plant-eating mammals such as zebras, cows, kangaroos, and elephants.

You might have to look closely to spot me. I have an excellent sense of smell, which helps me locate fresh piles of dung. Male insects of my species are so competitive, an entire dung pad can disappear within three hours! They try to impress future mates by creating the fanciest ball of dung. How romantic is that?

Some species in my family live underground in tunnels. The females dig the tunnels, and lay eggs in dung that is shoved down the tunnel by male beetles. The babies, called *grubs*, are born into a ready-made cafeteria. *Yum!*

Males spend their days sculpting dung balls to roll into the underground chamber. Some species prefer to set up housekeeping in a nice fresh pile of waste, rather than underground. That's where I live—in a big pile of poop. I lay eggs there, and my babies are born into a warm, smelly home.

Dung supplies certain bacteria and other nutrients that I need to survive. Dung also attracts extra treats—flies! God gave me a powerful set of jaws for tearing open old, dried heaps of dung and munching crunchy flies. I have a special purpose in life—to rid the countryside of dung, kill flies, and enrich the soil.

God thought of everything when he created me—**Dung Beetle.**

More on the Web

Schools in Australia are taking part in a project called Dung Beetle Mania. Learn more about this unusual insect at their website.

http://www.austmus.gov.au/biodiversity/dungbeetle/more/index.htm

Tell a Friend

Our size doesn't matter. Our age doesn't matter. God made each of us with a special purpose in mind—like the dung beetle.

In the Old Testament we read about a fire that burned the city gates of Jerusalem. One of the gates was called Dung Gate. Read about a man named Nehemiah, whose job it was to inspect the gates, in Nehemiah 2:13.

Read About It

"Work at everything you do with all your heart."—Colossians 3:23

Pray About It

I want to know the plan you have for my life, Lord. Help me to hear and obey your voice.

BLOOMIN' AND FUMIN'

Nobody makes a vase big enough to hold me. I am the biggest flower in the whole world! My petals grow to one and a half feet long and one inch thick! I grow on the Sumatra Island of Indonesia

Before my life began, rodents and small mammals nibbled at the flowers of one of my relatives, scattering its seeds across the vast forest floor. One of those seeds germinated in the root or stem of a thick, sturdy vine that snakes across the floor of tropical forests. The seed absorbed nutrients directly from the vine, but did not grow leaves like most plants.

After about 18 months, something peculiar happened. A small brown bud appeared. The bud took another 18 months to reach maturity. God provided the exact amount of water it needed to bloom. Too much or too little water will prevent me from blossoming. A successful bloom began when I fanned my five or six red, blotchy petals.

You will not have to wait in a long line to smell my blossom—

guaranteed! Sometimes referred to as a "corpse flower," it sends out a sickening stench like rotting meat, which attracts carrion flies—a type of fly that usually shows up to feast on dead flesh.

God thought of everything when he created me—**Rafflesia Arnoldi.**

More on the Web

Want to see a full-blown photo of a rafflesia arnoldi plant? Point your browser to:

http://www.emp.pdx.edu/htliono/images/p8.jpg

Tell a Friend

The Bible speaks of another kind of fragrance, and says that we can have that same sweet smell, too. When we live in a way that pleases God, our lives reflect his love to others.

Read About It

"You are the children that God dearly loves. So be just like him. Lead a life of love, just as Christ did. He loved us. He gave himself up for us. He was a sweet-smelling offering and sacrifice to God."
—Ephesians 5:1, 2

Pray About It

Thank you, Jesus, for offering up your life as a sweet-smelling sacrifice. Help others to see that you make a difference in my life.

Once it blooms, my flower only lasts for three to five days before it starts to rot.

BIRD WITH A CRASH HELMET

If I were a driver in your neighborhood, I would receive a speeding ticket. I have been clocked at cruising speeds of between 40 and 68 miles per hour. I am the fastest bird on record. Imagine that—me, the speediest bird in the whole world. But who's bragging?

I am easy to identify from a distance. A black cap of feathers hugs my head like a crash helmet—a perfect outfit for a bird with my reputation, don't you think? A mustache-shaped design of dark feathers decorates my beak.

I'm a speedy flier, but I took my time choosing a mate. My mate and I will live together our entire lives—about 15 years. Our nest sits on a tall cliff overlooking a river. If we had not been able to find a safe location for our nest, we would have chosen the top of a tall building in the middle of a busy city.

God gave me quick reactions and a keen eye to spot prey from a long way off. I am able to identify ducks, pheasants, blackbirds, and pigeons from five miles away! I dive full speed ahead in a deep plunge, catching them off guard. The sheer speed of our impact usually kills them instantly. I then swoop below a falling bird, and grab it with my long, fierce claws, called *talons*. My talons are sharp, which helps me hang onto my catch during my flight home.

God thought of everything when he created me—**Peregrine Falcon.**

More on the Web

Track peregrine falcons in the wild at this amazing website!

http://www.mb.ec.gc.ca/nature/endspecies/peregrine/index.en.html

Tell a Friend

When problems swoop down to grab you, are you easily thrown off course? Share how you handled a recent problem with God's help.

Read About It

"The Lord is a place of safety for those who have been beaten down. He keeps them safe in times of trouble." —Psalms 9:9

Pray About It

I am never outside your reach, Lord. Thank you for always watching over me.

Even though I have excellent vision, the Bible names one thing I cannot see. Read Job 28:1-7.

iTSY-BITSY SPIDER—NOT!

Y ou won't find me tiptoeing daintily across a web, because . . . *I'm bigger than a dinner plate!* If you guessed that I am the world's biggest spider, you're right. I'm covered in blondish-brown hair, and I'm related to the tarantula. My home is a burrow in the damp, marshy area of a South American jungle.

A critter my size has a gigantic appetite. I've heard a report that I eat birds, but trust me—it rarely happens. Birds are too hard for me to catch! My favorite potluck consists of frogs, small snakes, lizards, beetles, and bats. I sneak up on my prey, pounce on them, and then bite them with poison-filled fangs. My method of attack has been compared to that of large jungle cats.

When I am disturbed, I let loose with a hissing noise that can be heard 15 feet away! I don't have a voice box like you, though; I make noise by rubbing my bristly legs together.

I usually save my hisses for intruders that are bigger than me, including humans.

If my hissing doesn't scare you into retreating, I have a special hair trick. God gave me the ability to shoot tiny barbed hairs into the air. Those sharp, bristly hairs will damage lungs, eyes, and skin. Hey, it's my only way of protecting myself against the giants of the world.

God thought of everything when he created me—**Goliath Bird-Eating Spider.**

More on the Web

To eyeball a close-up photo of a Goliath bird-eating spider, point your browser to Tarantula.com:

http://www.tarantulas.com/goliath.asp

Tell a Friend

The Goliath bird-eating spider is known for its quick attack. Words are sometimes like that, too—quick and hurtful. God provides self-control at just the right moment, though, when we call on him.

Read About It

"A man who is wise says gracious things. But a foolish person is destroyed by what his own lips speak." —Ecclesiastes 10:12

Some South Americans eat tarantulas as a good source of protein!

Pray About It

Lord, help me to think before I speak, and to treat others the way I would like to be treated.

A MELON-EATING LAWN MOWER

I'm a large rodent, just like a guinea pig or a mouse, except I bet you'll never run into a 140-pound guinea pig or mouse! My scientific name, *hydrochoerus*, means "water pig." I measure over four feet long and two feet tall, and live in a family of about 20 members called a *troop*.

We spend cool nights searching for food. We are herbivores, which means we only eat plants. Give me a salad of grasses, roots, and bark, topped off with a dessert of melons, and I'm one happy herbivore. I never sleep for long; I prefer naps all through the day. I will live to a ripe old age of eight to ten years, as long as jaguars and crocodiles don't turn me into breakfast!

I am skilled at living both in and out of water. God designed my head with small eyes and nostrils on top, similar to an alligator. My front legs are shorter than my hind legs, with webbed toes. The design of my legs help me to paddle water or hurry across the bottom of the swamp in a running motion.

The South American Indians refer to me as Master of Grasses, because I can turn an empty-looking field into a feast. Can you imagine the fun I'd have "mowing" your lawn?

God thought of everything when he created me—**Capybara**.

More on the Web

The capybara is the largest rodent in the world. Learn more about this amazing animal, and print a detailed drawing for coloring or painting, compliments of Enchanted Learning:

http://www.enchantedlearning.com/subjects/mammals/rodent/Capybaraprintout.shtml

Tell a Friend

The capybara is a master at "mowing" a field. What types of things do you do well? Have you considered how God can use your skills? Share your dream with a trusted friend and pray together.

Read About It

"Find your delight in the Lord. Then he will give you everything your heart really wants."—Psalm 37:4

I'm a social animal that communicates by whistling and barking.

Pray About It

Lord, thank you for listening to my hopes and dreams. Help me to use the skills and abilities you have given me.

45

COOL, CALM, AND STRIPED

I am known for my beautiful striped coat. Certain members of my large family are striped from head to toe, but not me. My striped pattern ends a ways down my sides, where my belly begins. My belly is snow-white. I have long ears and a large, square flap of skin under my throat, called a dewlap.

During colder months, I seek shelter in caves or wooded ravines. The rest of the year I live in mountain grasslands at an elevation of around 6,500 feet. During warmer months, you can find me grazing in the rugged country east of the Namid Desert in Africa.

God knew that I'd need an efficient way to keep cool. He fashioned a shiny black and white coat for me, with special hair that deflects over 70 percent of the mid-afternoon heat!

My coat also provides excellent camouflage from my predators: leopards, lions, cheetahs, hunting dogs, and spotted hyenas. When I stand behind a tree with jutting branches, my beautiful black and white stripes blend in with my surroundings. In the evenings when the light grows dim, other animals can't see me.

God thought of everything when he created me —**Mountain Zebra**.

More on the Web

How much do you know about zebras? Take this quiz at National Geographic.com:

http://www.nationalgeographic.com/world/amfacts/zebra_q1.html

Tell a Friend

The mountain zebra knows exactly where and how to stand in order to blend in with its surroundings. As Christians, we can do just the opposite. Instead of "standing in the shadows," we can ask God to give us opportunities to boldly share his love with others. We can make a difference in their lives.

Read About It

"Don't let anyone look down on you because you are young. Set an example for the believers in what you say and in how you live. Also set an example in how you love and in what you believe."
—1 Timothy 4:12

Different types of zebras have different patterns of stripes. Researchers now believe that stripes are more than just camouflage. They help individual zebras to recognize other family members.

Pray About It

Lord, it's easy to blend in with the crowd, but I don't want to hide my faith! Thank you for helping me show your love through my words and actions.

THREE CHEERS FOR THE FISHTRONAUT!

Have you taken a long walk lately? I wonder how many humans consider what it takes to walk, run, and jump without falling. Imagine what it would be like to lose your balance every time you tied your shoe or stepped out of a car. God knew the importance of balance, and created your ears with a special fluid-filled canal. Tiny hairs sense every little movement. Each ear adjusts your balance according to the position you are in.

Well, guess what? Scientists discovered that my balancing system is much like a human's. They even decided to use me in a special experiment to prove their hunch. In 1998, one of my fish friends and I were plucked out of the waters near Woods Hole, Massachusetts. We became fishtronauts on the Space Shuttle Columbia!

Who would have thought a fish like me would ever fly three million miles into space? They wanted to see whether my pal and I would lose our sense of balance in a place without gravity. Would we be able to tell up from down, or would we get dizzy and topple over?

Being a famous fishtronaut was the high point of my life. You see, I have always been known as the ugliest, laziest fish around—a worthless creature in a big, cold sea. My Creator didn't see it that way, though. Out of all the fish in the sea, I was chosen for a special honor.

God thought of everything when he created me—**Oyster Toadfish.**

More on the Web

The ocean might seem like a vast, silent place, but did you know that fish make noise? Listen to an oyster toadfish:

http://personal.ecu.edu/spraguem/fish/opstau.html.

Tell a Friend

If a creature like the oyster toadfish has an important purpose in life, imagine how God can use each of us! Ask God to help you develop the abilities he has given you.

Read About It

"So God created the great creatures of the ocean. He created every living and moving thing that fills the waters. He created all kinds of them."—Genesis 1:21

My head is broad and flat, and some say I look like a gigantic tadpole, or baby frog.

Pray About It

Dear Lord, give me a heart of thankfulness so I can praise you for making me just the way I am.

THE RAINFOREST STRANGLER

The rainforest is my home. I stand nearly 70 feet tall, and measure eight feet around my hollow trunk, but I wasn't always this size. Years ago, a bird deposited a seed from a fig it had eaten. The seed passed through the bird's digestive system, and landed on a mossy branch. It quickly germinated, and began sending out vines.

God provided lots of sunshine there at the top of my tall host tree. He protected me from fire and flood. Plant-eating animals could not nibble on my young roots up there, either. Year by year, my roots grew thicker and longer. They circled the tree like tangled limbs. I squeezed the tree trunk so tightly, it quit growing!

As I grew, I sent out a thick umbrella of leaves to shade my host tree. It eventually died from lack of sunshine.

I used its hollow, lifeless trunk like an ivy growing on a lattice. God has given me a special job. I produce fruit year round, which provides nourishment for birds and mammals when other food is scarce.

I am an important part of the food chain in the rainforest.

As fruit-eating birds feast on my figs, the seeds pass through their digestive tract, and are planted on other tree branches. New saplings start, and the process begins all over again.

God thought of everything when he created me—**Strangler Fig.**

More on the Web

Lamington National Park in Australia provides facts and photos of a strangler fig:

http://lamington.nrsm.uq.edu.au/docs/Plant/Fig.htm

Tell a Friend

The strangler fig has a purpose. It feeds animals at times when they might otherwise go hungry. God created you with a purpose, too—a perfect plan for your life!

Read About It

"God is working in you. He wants your plans and your acts to be in keeping with his good purpose."—Philippians 2:13

Of the 800 or so fig species, about 200 of them wrap around a host tree and strangle it.

Pray About It

Thank you, Lord, for creating me with a special purpose in mind! Help me to understand it, so I can walk the path you have charted for my life.

KEEPING COOL IN THE SONORA

Who needs cool blue lakes with all this sand? Here in the Sonora Desert, my friends and I keep cool by burrowing into a sand dune. The temperature 12 inches deep is often a whopping 50 degrees cooler than the surface sand. It's like changing from summer to winter in one quick leap. My snout works like a shovel and I have a muscular neck, which helps me maneuver under the dune quickly.

God planned a way to protect my eyes and ears from all this sand. My eyes lock shut, thanks to tiny interlocking scales. Scaly ear flaps keep sand from filling up my ears, too. Nose valves save me from suffocation, and an upper lip overhangs like a miniature windshield.

I'm most famous for my unusual toes, which work like snowshoes. Covered with scales, they increase traction while I'm dashing across soft sand. If I can't outrun a predator, no problem; I just brake and burrow!

Temperatures in the desert can change drastically from sunrise to sunset. During milder temperatures, I stay above ground and blend in with my surroundings. My back is covered with bumpy, velvety scales that mimic the color and texture of sand. I have a built-in thermometer, called a *parietal eye*. It's not a typical eye, but a sensor that alerts me when my body needs to cool down. When my temperature reaches a dangerous level, I dive under the sand and cool off quickly.

God thought of everything when he created me—**Sonoran Fringe-Toed Lizard.**

More on the Web

Here's my family album. Aren't we a handsome group of spiny lizards?

http://www.enature.com/fieldguide/showSpecies_LI.asp?imageID=19326

Tell a Friend

God taught the Sonoran fringe-toed lizard how to escape from its enemies. In the Bible, God gives his people clear instructions on how to run from sin, too. It's the best handbook you'll ever own!

Read About It

"The name of the Lord is like a strong tower. Godly people run to it and are safe."—Proverbs 18:10

Pray About It

Your way is always best, Lord. Help me to make good choices.

My family name is phrynosomatidae. How's that for a mouthful?

WELCOME TO MY FRUIT STAND!

I'm famous along the slopes of the Andes, because I am the only bear to live in South America. You could say I'm king of the hill! I tip the scales at 250 to 300 pounds, but am still smaller than most bears. I sport a shaggy reddish-brown coat decorated by a cream-colored area around my mouth, throat, and chest. But my real claim to fame is the yellow rings circling my eyes.

God must have thought about how much time I would be spending up a tree. He custom-designed special claws for climbing. Sometimes I reach the top of a tree, only to discover that the fruit isn't ripe yet. No problem! I just build a tree stand out of dry branches and wait. There I will stay for days at a time, until the fruit is ripe enough to eat.

In addition to fruit, I like the taste of shrubs, honey, sugarcane, small birds, rodents, and insects. I've been spotted climbing a cactus to eat fresh spring flowers at the top, too.

My jaws are strong. They allow me the pleasure of tough treats like tree bark, too. I strip the bark off a tree the way you strip the peel off a banana (except you don't eat your banana peel).

I don't hibernate like other bears. That's because I can find plenty of food any season, so why sleep when there's a feast around every corner? Fortunately, I am not a picky eater. I eat foods that other animals refuse.

God thought of everything when he created me—**Spectacled Bear.**

More on the Web

Learn about the lifestyle of a spectacled bear at the Lincoln Park Zoo:

http://www.lpzoo.com/tour/factsheets/mammals/spec_bear.html

Tell a Friend

The spectacled bear adapts well to change, season after season, and we can, too. The Bible assures us that life's circumstances may change, but Jesus remains the same.

Read About It

"Jesus Christ is the same yesterday, today, and forever."—Hebrews 13:8

Read how one Bible character wrestled with a bear and won in 1 Samuel 17:33-37.

Pray About It

Lord, it's nice to know that you never change! Thank you for helping me through times of change, and for understanding how I feel.

55

I'M NOT CRAZY, JUST A LITTLE CUCKOO

People run from wasps, or swat at them, but my very life depends on them. I am a parasite—an insect that feeds off of other insects. I am also a wasp myself, which makes my life as a parasite a bit peculiar.

Some people call me a ruby wasp or jewel wasp because of my colors. I'm bright metallic blue, green, or red. You won't catch me standing still for long, because I'm small, fast, and sneaky.

I hide near nests of wasps, bees, and certain other insects, such as sawflies and stick insects. I spy on them until the host leaves, then hurry inside and lay my eggs there.

Before I leave, I help myself to a snack of dead bugs—like a burglar raiding a refrigerator. Some of my favorite snacks are aphids, caterpillars, or spiders. There's a ready supply of them in a wasp's nest, since that is what wasps drag inside to feed their babies.

God gave me a strong covering, called a *cuticle*, in case an insect tries to attack me. It is thick, hard, and dotted with tiny pits. The underside of my abdomen is flexible, so I can easily roll up into a ball and play dead. I rarely sting, but if I am threatened, I have a small stinger that will stun an enemy.

God thought of everything when he created me—**Cuckoo Wasp.**

More on the Web

Compare the colorful cuckoo wasp to six other types of these busy insects.

http://www.everythingabout.net/articles/biology/animals/arthropods/insects/wasps/cuckoo_wasp

Tell a Friend

The cuckoo wasp is a parasite. All it does is take, take, take! God planned friendship to work the opposite. Give of yourself to a friend-ship, and it will bless you in countless ways!

Read About It

"A friend loves at all times. He is there to help when trouble comes." —Proverbs 17:17

There are approximately 3,000 species of cuckoo wasps throughout the world, including about 230 in the United States and Canada.

Pray About It

Dear God, thank you for my friends. Show me ways I can bless their lives this week.

HIPPITY-HOPPITY ME

I'd invite you into my cozy, grass-lined home in Australia, but you're too big to squeeze down five feet of tunnels. I dug the burrow myself, according to God's blueprint. My sharp claws worked quickly, digging and smoothing out corridors. I'm at home here in Australia, but other members of my family live in meadows and at the edge of forests in the northern United States and Canada.

Please don't compare me to those drab gray field mice. *Harrumph!* I'm much prettier, if I do say so myself. My fur coat is two-toned: dark on top and yellowish-brown on my soft belly. A bold stripe runs along my sides where the two colors meet.

You won't find me snooping around your garage or running in the attic during cold winter months. I sleep nine months of every year. After my hibernation period, I awaken during the warmer months of summer. Summertime is my busy season. I make up for nine months of inactivity by feasting on insects, leaves and stems, seeds, and berries.

At night, you'll find me hopping around my territory. That's right; I *hop!* God knew I'd need long, thin hind legs to spring me forward. He fashioned my tail extra-long, to help me keep my balance. My body measures about four inches, but my tail is even longer. Altogether, I'm an eight-inch "mighty mouse."

God thought of everything when he created me—**Spinifex Hopping Mouse.**

More on the Web

Every now and then, a sneaky photographer snaps a picture of me:

http://www.tesag.jcu.edu.au/subjects/ge3555/GE3555aridgeog/sld021.htm

Tell a Friend

God taught the hopping mouse how to hop, and where to find food at night. He teaches us, too, through his Word—the Bible. Share what the Bible means to you.

Read About It

"Trust in the Lord with all your heart. Do not depend on your own understanding. In all your ways remember him. Then he will make your paths smooth and straight." —Proverbs 3:5, 6

It's not unusual for me to share my burrow with other species of mice like me.

Pray About It

God, thank you for listening to my prayers and for keeping me on track.

YOU CAN CALL ME "SWEETIE"

I live underground in a fancy ant's nest—a maze of tunnels and domed chambers connected to one narrow vertical hallway. It doesn't look like a typical ant hill, because it isn't a hill at all. Look closely, and you'll see ants coming and going through a narrow circular opening at ground level.

I'm a *replete*—a worker ant. Worker ants come in all sizes, and I belong to a group that is physically different from the others. God knew that I'd need a stretchy abdomen, called a *crop*. My crop serves as one of many storage tanks for the colony. During cool nights, I fill my crop with sweet nectar from flowers. Sometimes I add water, fats, and body fluid from insect prey, too.

Each tribe has a unique *colony odor*. If I meet another ant during my nightly adventure, I quickly check to see if it is one of my nest-mates. If a fellow ant from my colony needs a quick energy snack, we exchange honey mouth-to-mouth.

I live with other honey-gathering repletes in a special chamber at the bottom of the nest. Our room is a pantry for the colony—a well-stocked source of food. When my supply of nectar runs low, I go hunting again. During the rainy season, our community never suffers from a lack of food, thanks to my stretchy storage tank!

God thought of everything when he created me—**Honey Ant**.

More on the Web
Explore a virtual ant encyclopedia!

http://ant.edb.miyakyo-u.ac.jp/INTRODUCTION/Gakken79E/Page_02.html

Tell a Friend
The honey ant quickly recognizes members of its family. The Bible teaches us how believers in Jesus can recognize each other, too. When we are living for Christ, our lives reflect his love.

Read About It
"No one has ever seen God. But if we love one another, God lives in us. His love is made complete in us."—1 John 4:12

Pray About It
Dear God, I want others to see how much I love you. Help me to live my life so they will see Christ through me.

The ant is a hard-working creature. Read what the Bible has to say about the ant in Proverbs 6:6.

VACUUM CLEANER OF THE SEA

I might look like a vegetable that belongs in a tossed green salad, but look closer. I'm actually a soft-bodied relative to the starfish and sand dollar. I make my home in the Galapagos Islands. Marine biologists think I'm pretty special. In fact, they say I help turn over as much as 90 percent of the sea floor! My sifting work helps keep the seabed healthy, but I can live for five to ten years at any water depth.

My body is decorated with tiny tube feet. They work like mini suction cups, called *tentacles*, attaching me firmly in place. As I move from place to place along the ocean's bottom, my tentacles keep me rooted in place. Without them, I would drift aimlessly through the water.

God designed another group of tube feet near my mouth. These tubes act as my arms, although they're called *feet*. They're constantly in motion, sweeping the water around me like tiny vacuum cleaners. They bend and sway, capturing tiny bits of food, keeping me plump and pampered.

If a bully of the sea approaches, I play dead. It's the only way I know how to protect myself. I disconnect my organs quickly, including my two breathing tubes. Nobody messes with me if they think I'm already dead. Little do they know that I can grow a whole new set of necessary organs in just a few weeks!

God thought of everything when he created me—**Sea Cucumber.**

More on the Web

Read about a sea cucumber "gold rush":

http://www.worldwildlife.org/galapagos/cucumber.cfm

Tell a Friend

The sea cucumber's tentacles help "root" it, so it does not float aimlessly through the water. The Bible does the same for us, by giving us good advice to follow. Aren't you glad we can trust in God's care?

Read About It

"Let us hold firmly to the hope we claim to have. The One who promised is faithful."—Hebrews 10:23

In some parts of the world, I am considered a delicacy. Would YOU eat me for lunch?

Pray About It

Heavenly Father, I want to follow you. Help me to hide your Word in my heart.

CAN YOU SPELL "HEADACHE"?

I am the only wild white sheep in the world. God created me with a thick coat for warmth. Each hair of my coat is hollow, insulating my body while I explore the alpine ridges, meadows, and steep, craggy cliffs of Alaska. Within hours of my birth, I was sure-footed enough to climb the steep slopes with my herd, because the bottoms of my hooves are lined with a spongy, rough pad. They help me grip the ledges and cliffs, where I run when I sense danger. I am light-footed and quick. From hoof to shoulder I measure about three feet, and weigh around 250 pounds.

Male members of my herd, called *rams*, butt heads in a fierce contest to see who is the strongest. We live together except for during the mating season, so it is important for us to understand who is in charge. We are thickheaded, thanks to God, who created our skulls with a double layer of bone. That extra layer prevents injury during our head-butting contests.

It takes about eight years to grow a full set of horns. My horns are made of *keratin*—the same substance you have in your fingernails! Each year's growth produces a ring pattern on my horns, much like the rings on a tree. Count the rings, and you will be able to figure my age.

God thought of everything when he created me—**Dall Sheep.**

More on the Web
How is a dall sheep's eating habits similar to a cow's?

http://www.enchantedlearning.com/subjects/mammals/sheep/Dallsheep.shtml

Tell a Friend
The dall sheep is sure-footed and strong. It faces its challenges head-on. When we face problems, the Bible has the answer we need. We can become as sure-footed as the dall sheep, by following the example Jesus set for us.

Read About It
"He gives me new strength. He guides me in the right paths for the honor of his name."—Psalm 23:3

Jesus tells about the joy in finding a lost sheep. Read the story in Luke 15: 3-7.

Pray About It
Father, I want to obey you. Help me to stay sure-footed in your Word.

A BARKING DUCK ON STILTS?

If you're ever trekking through the Andes mountains of southern Ecuador, listen closely. Do you hear a barking sound? That's me calling!

Now, barking might not sound like such a big deal—except for one tiny detail: I happen to be a bird! I was discovered by an *ornithologist* (a person who studies birds) in the Andes Mountains of Ecuador in June 1998. He stopped in his tracks after hearing my strange bark. When I refused to come out into a clearing, he decided to trick me out of hiding. He tape recorded my barking voice, thinking that I would respond to another bird's call. Then he turned up the volume and waited.

Sure enough, I did think that another bird was calling. I hurried to within 25 feet of the tape recorder, where this enthusiastic bird-lover could get a good look at me. Can you imagine the thrill of discovering a new species of bird?

I am a member of the *antbird* family—birds that follow army ants through the dense forest. Like a hungry traveler picking up leftover fruit in an orchard, I forage for insects left behind by armies of ants. God gave me springy legs that help me bounce from snack to snack, like a pogo stick. Because I move quickly, ants don't have a chance to hop aboard my long, skinny legs.

God thought of everything when he created me—**Giant Antpitta.**

More on the Web

Explore the world of antbirds through this fantastic scavenger hunt at Smithsonian.com:

http://www.bergen.org/Smithsonian/Antbirds/

Tell a Friend

God gave the giant antpitta a unique way to communicate. Every person has a one-of-a-kind voice, too. What does your voice say about you? Are you patient and kind, or impatient and demanding?

Of all the birds discovered in the past 50 years, I am the biggest. I guess that makes me a celebrity!

Read About It

"There is a time to be silent. And there's a time to speak."—Ecclesiastes 3:7

Pray About It

Help me to think before I speak, dear God. I want to use my voice to bless others.

A MEAN, LEAN FISHING MACHINE

I'm not interested in munching my dinner from a little blue dish in the corner of a warm kitchen. No, thank you! I am a 29-pound cat who would rather leap into cold, swampy water than wait for a can opener. God created me to live wild and free.

A swampy region of Asia is my home. It's a perfect spot for satisfying a big appetite like mine. I fish the rivers and streams here, but prefer the still waters of a marsh to swift rivers. God gave me quick reactions, and it's a good thing! I have to know the exact second to leap into the water after my next meal, or I'll lose out.

I have special feet for swimming—four webbed feet with extra-long claws. My sharp claws are my fishhooks. I can either grab a passing fish with my fishhooks, or jump in headfirst and snatch it with my jaws, like a bear catching salmon. Once I land a slippery, wiggly fish, a claw makes an excellent dinner fork.

I am considered the best swimmer of all the cats in Asia. I'm not apt to curl up on anyone's lap for a neck scratching, though. I'm all business, and you won't ever catch me trying to purr my way into anybody's heart

God thought of everything when he created me—**Fishing Cat.**

More on the Web

View a photo of a mean, lean fishing cat at this educational website:

http://elib.cs.berkeley.edu/cgi/img_query?enlarge=0000+0000+0901+0661

Tell a Friend

God equipped the fishing cat with everything it needs to care of itself. He taught it how to fish and survive in the swamps of Asia. What has God taught you to do well? How are you using your unique talents and abilities?

Read About It

"Work at everything you do with all your heart. Work as if you were working for the Lord." —Colossians 3:23

Pray About It

Lord, thank you for giving me special talents and abilities. Help me to use them wisely.

My double-layered fur coat keeps me warm even in cold water.

EYE TO EYE

You will not find me fluttering around the flowers in your backyard. My home is the deep tropical forest of Central America. Like many rainforest creatures, I am a one of the larger members of my family.

Sometimes I am confused with the owl moth, but we're really quite different. Moths fly around only at night; while butterflies like me fly during daylight hours. My wings act as little solar heaters, by continuing to warm my body long after I leave my sunny perch.

When resting, moths lie with their wings flat. Not me! I tuck my wings close to my sides, which exposes only my underside. I am easily identified by large *eye spots* on the bottom of my colorful wings. When I sense danger nearby, I flash my fake eyes. Those dark spots scare away intruders, who mistakenly believe they are the eyes of a wild beast.

My appetite for tropical fruit has earned me a bad reputation with local farmers. Back in my caterpillar days, a few hundred friends and

I could damage an entire crop of bananas. However, my plain brown caterpillar days are long gone. You should see me now! I'm a brilliant powdery blue color, with a wing span of around eight inches. I have relatives whose wings boast shades of gray, brown, orange, and purple. Together, we create a spectacular show around dusk, when we feed off ripe bananas and other fruits of the tropical forest.

God thought of everything when he created me—**Great Owl Butterfly.**

More on the Web
Here are two different types of owl butterflies:

http://www.butterflies.org/lvstk.cfm?lvstkID=22

Tell a Friend
The great owl butterfly keeps others at a distance as a means of protecting itself, but God gives us human friends to share our lives. Have you told your friends how much they mean to you?

Read About It
"A friend loves at all times. He is there to help when trouble comes."—Proverbs 17:17

Pray About It
Thank you, God, for the wonderful gift of friendship! Show me ways to help my friend feel treasured.

My life span lasts from a few days to about eight months.

71

SINGING THE BLUES

Have you ever wanted to give your room a whole new look? Same here!

However, take it from me—a well-decorated living space does not happen overnight. It requires a lot of time, planning, and effort.

Here in the misty rainforest of New Guinea, I get my name from the thatched structure, called a *bower*, I build as part of my courtship ritual. A bower is not a nest, but a special place where I hope to meet a mate. I am a master architect, and my fancy bowers are so beautiful, bird lovers have photographed and studied them.

God gave me the instinct to fashion a U-shaped bower from strong twigs, leaves, and moss. Once the walls of my bower are set securely in place, the fun begins! I search high and low for blue objects to use as decorations in my new room. You won't find pinks or reds in my bower. I collect only blue feathers, flowers, berries, and shells, plus any shiny trinkets I can find. Before settlers arrived,

I settled for blue items from nature. Now I'll take anything with a blue tint, from blue bottle caps and ink pens to clothing and paper.

While waiting to attract a mate, I stand guard over my fancy blue bower, so other young males don't steal my decorations. I also pass the time by painting my walls with a special mixture of crushed berries, saliva, and charcoal.

God thought of everything when he created me—**Satin Bowerbird.**

More on the Web

Listen to a satin bowerbird from Australia at this site filled with fun facts.

http://lamington.nrsm.uq.edu.au/docs/Birds/Sbow.htm

Tell a Friend

The satin bowerbird uses ordinary objects to create something beautiful. God can take an ordinary life, too, and turn it into something bright and beautiful. How is he decorating your life?

Read About It

"The same Lord is Lord of all. He richly blesses everyone who calls on him."—Romans 10:12

For nine months of every year, I am either building or remodeling my bower.

Pray About It

Lord, sometimes I feel very ordinary, but I know that to you, I am EXTRAordinary! Thank you for loving and encouraging me.

RHINO WITH AN ATTITUDE

One-fifth of all the world's species are beetles, so I am in good company. I belong to the large family of scarab beetles. Some of my cousins live in North America, but are not as big as those of us who live in tropical forests. Although I'm harmless to humans, if you spotted my eight-inch frame lurking in the corner of your patio, you might run for cover!

My wings are encased in a tough, bony covering, like an armor. If I were to get trapped underwater, I would survive by trapping air under my hard shell. God added breathing holes to my armor, too.

Sword-shaped horns curve over my head. We males use our horns in combat when we compete for a mate. We also fight for the best nesting site. I have a third horn, which sits in the middle of my head. It is shaped like the horn of a rhinoceros.

Each of my six legs sport a pair of claws called *tarsi*. They're so strong, I'm able to hang onto trees. Once I get a good grip, I'm nearly impossible to pry off.

God had a special reason for creating my family. Larvae provide a valuable food source for other animals. Adult beetles chew decomposing wood with our massive jaws. We help recycle material on the forest floor.

God thought of everything when he created me—**Rhinoceros Beetle.**

More on the Web

See why I'm called the biggest beetle in the world!

http://members.aol.com/Lecdyatis2/occi.html

Tell a Friend

The rhinoceros beetle's armor comes in handy in difficult situations. Likewise, the Bible says that everyone who believes in Jesus has armor, too. Fully dressed in our spiritual armor, we can stand up courageously for our Savior.

Read About It

"So put on all of God's armor. Evil days will come. But you will be able to stand up to anything. And after you have done everything you can, you will still be standing."—Ephesians 6:13

Pray About It

Dear God, thank you for protecting me with spiritual armor. Give me courage to live for you.

When I fly, I make a whirring sound like a helicopter.

RIDING THE WAVES

Imagine what it would be like to float across the ocean without a ship. I am a drift seed, and that is exactly what happened to me.

I grew in a paper-like seedpod on a long climbing vine called a *liana.* The vine hung from a tall canopy of trees in Central America. At the end of each vine bloomed a beautiful flower.

Inside the pod, I was covered with dense black hair. My fuzzy coating eventually wore off, exposing a tough, dark brown outer shell that looked and felt like wood. God made sure that it was waterproof, too.

My journey to the sea began when I fell from my seedpod to the forest floor. Heavy rains carried me to a river, where I bobbed along for several days. I reached a sandy beach, where the high tide finally swept me out to sea. There I joined thousands of drift seeds riding the waves. Some were shaped differently than me, but we all had one thing in common: God knew our final destination.

I ended up on a tropical beach, thousands of miles away from my rainforest home. If God had not planned ahead, I would have sunk to the bottom of the ocean. Inside my woody shell, He had placed a special air pocket. That little bit of air made me float!

God thought of everything when he created me—**Sea Bean.**

More on the Web

Are sea beans really beans? Read more about drift seeds here:

http://www.seabean.com/what.htm

Tell a Friend

Just like a sea bean, God has equipped each of us for our journey through life. He planned every detail, and knows our comings and our goings. He cares about what happens to us!

Read About It

"The Lord will watch over your life no matter where you go, both now and forever."—Psalm 121:8

Pray About It

Lord, you know me better than I know myself. Thank you for equipping me perfectly for the life you have given me.

Scientists studied one drift seed and determined that it had traveled 15,000 miles!

GET A GRIP!

I'm rabbit-sized, and wear a thick brownish coat that blends well with the African savanna. I weigh about as much as a small sack of potatoes, and am 19 inches long. God knew that I would spend my life climbing rocks, so on the padded soles of each foot he created a flap. The flaps pull back, forming suction cups! My front feet have four toes, and flat-bottomed nails that look like small hooves.

My body does not adjust well to changes in temperature, so I avoid grazing when it's too hot or too cold. My family and I sunbathe by day, and huddle together for warmth at night. All 25 of us squeeze into our cozy rock crevice, and pile atop one another like a stack of hairy pancakes.

When we graze out on the open plains, we eat quickly to lessen the chance that we'll be attacked. We communicate well, using various sounds. When I was a newborn, I spoke with mews, like a lost kitten. Now I relay messages by yelping, grunting, and when alarmed—

squeaking loudly.

My upper teeth are triangle-shaped, and look like little tusks. My lower teeth are like the teeth of a comb, and come in handy for grooming. I am not a fussy eater, and devour almost everything in sight, even plants that might be poisonous to other animals.

God thought of everything when he created me—**Rock Hyrax.**

More on the Web

Utah's Hogle Zoo has an adorable picture of its resident rock hyrax:

http://www.xmission.com/~hoglezoo/mammals/hyrax.htm

Tell a Friend

The members of the rock hyrax family understand each other because they are good communicators. They say exactly what they mean, and are good listeners. How well do you communicate with others when you are worried, happy, or afraid?

To avoid an attack while we're grazing, my family and I position ourselves in a fan pattern so we can keep a watchful eye out for party crashers.

Read About It

"Turn all your worries over to him. He cares about you."—1 Peter 5:7

Pray About It

Lord, I know I can tell you anything and you will listen. Thank you for hearing my prayers, even before I speak them.

I SMELL TROUBLE

What is bigger than a robin, but smaller than a computer? Me! I'm a national symbol in New Zealand—a small, flightless bird that locals refer to as their "honorary mammal." My family includes African ostriches, the rheas of South America, and the moa of New Zealand, which is now extinct.

I hardly resemble a bird at all. At the tip of my beak sit a pair of nostrils. I don't just peck at my food; I sniff it. I sniff and snort after spiders, earthworms, grubs, and fallen fruits before I eat them. I also use my beak to sniff out danger.

Tiny, two-inch wings look silly on such a plump, feathery body. I can't fly, but I *can* outrun a human. If a possum, pig, or ferret wanders near, watch out! My three-toed, clawed feet are weapons. I use them to kick and slash.

Like many birds, I mate for life. My mate cares for the nest and eggs, even to the point of not eating. Eggs take around 80 days to hatch, and a male can drop a third of his body weight during his time in the nest. God provides a special reserve of yolk in the belly of a new chick until it is three weeks old. It then leaves the nest with its father to search for food.

God thought of everything when he created me—**Kiwi Bird.**

More on the Web

Get acquainted the kiwi bird and other wildlife of New Zealand:

http://www.kcc.org.nz/factsheets.htm

Tell a Friend

The flightless kiwi bird does not sit around flapping its useless wings. It is too busy running, hunting, and caring for its family. God can turn our lives into something beautiful when we just ask.

Read About It

"We all have gifts. They differ in keeping with the grace that God has given each of us."—Romans 12:6

I lay one of the largest eggs of any bird my size. I am chicken-sized, but my eggs are as big as an ostrich's egg!

Pray About It

Help me to use the gifts you have given me, dear Lord. I want my life to make a difference in your world.

DON'T EXPECT ME TO QUACK!

When you're hungry, you head to the refrigerator, right? Not me; I dive deep and swim to the bottom of a river, where I feed at dawn and again at dusk. My warm, wooly undercoat and furry, waterproof outer layer are God's way of protecting my skin. The two layers work together to trap air to keep me warm and dry, even though I spend hours underwater.

My leathery, duck-like bill is perfect for stirring up mud in my search for shellfish, worms, and insects. Charged with tiny sensory nerve endings, it alerts me to predators nearby. My bill also helps me navigate around obstacles like rocks. I look like a duck, but don't expect me to quack!

I swim with webbed front feet, and use my hind feet for steering and braking. God designed my hind feet to fold back against my tail when I'm not using them. A long, bristly tail helps me steer and keep my balance. If a human or animal tries to catch me, I zap them with a poisonous spur on my hind leg.

I don't hibernate like many animals. But during the colder months, I do take naps that can last up to six days! My body temperature falls in order to conserve energy, and I am inactive during that time.

God thought of everything when he created me—**Platypus.**

More on the Web
Check out 13 poses of a playful platypus:

http://www.21century.com.au/environment/platphotos.htm

Tell a Friend
God keeps the platypus warm, dry, well-fed, and protected. He provides everything we need, too. When's the last time you counted your blessings and named them one by one?

Read About It
"He has shown kindness by giving you rain from heaven. He gives you crops in their seasons. He provides you with plenty of food. He fills your hearts with joy." —Acts 14:17

When I dig my burrow, I fold back the skin of my webbed forefeet to expose claws.

Pray About It
Lord, you watch over me from morning to night, and even while I sleep. Thank you for blessing me so!

A FISH OUT OF WATER

I am a vertebrate—I have a backbone. I also have fins and breathe through gills. I am a fish, but also a member of the Goby family of amphibians. My home is located along a large bay near Japan. Members of my family live on tropical shorelines from Africa through Southeast Asia and the Philippines to Japan.

I'm a favorite subject of photographers, who love to capture my flip-flopping, leaping courtship dance. If they persist, I'll run away by pushing myself along with my front fins. When I feel cornered, I'll dive into the mud. Photographers who don't give up their chase often end up knee-deep in the gooey mess. Now *that's* a picture!

How can a creature that breathes through its gills survive underneath all that ooze? God knows the secrets of my existence. He gave me an amazing collection of spongy sacs near my gills. As I breathe through my gills underwater, I absorb and store oxygen in my sacs. Like a diver with an oxygen tank, I can survive several minutes on land or buried in mud.

I need to roll in puddles often, to keep my gills moist and free of mud. While bathing, I keep a close watch out for birds like herons, who consider me fast food. Most fish see clearly only underwater, but my bulging eyes see well on dry land for about 30 yards—almost a third of the length of a football field!

God thought of everything when he created me—**Mudskipper.**

More on the Web

Here's your chance to eyeball a mudskipper!

http://www.wiljo.nu/images/fisksidae/mudskipper2.htm

Tell a Friend

Like the mudskipper, God knows all about you. He knew you long before you were born. God designed your exact eye color, hair, and height long before you drew your first breath!

Read About It

"From the time I was born, you took good care of me. Ever since I came out of my mother's body, you have been my God."—Psalm 22:10

Pray About It

Lord, you have loved me forever. Help me to trust you more each day.

One of my mud-skipping relatives knows how to climb trees!

QUAKIN' IN MY ROOTS!

I began life as a single tree. Pioneer settlers to the United States nicknamed me "quakey", because my leaves would tremble at the slightest breeze. More recently, I have gained the nickname of "Pando", which means, "I spread." Located south of the Wasatch Mountains in Utah, I am the biggest tree of my kind on record.

Passersby may think I'm just a normal grove of trees, but I am actually one 6,600-ton tree, spread across 200 acres! Biologists have studied tissue samples from all of the trees in my grove and yep—I'm their mom!

Most trees reproduce by wind-blown seeds, but God planned another way for me to spread. New plants called *suckers* grew straight out of my roots. As the suckers grew upward toward the light, my strong roots provided nutrients and moisture, like a mother nursing a baby. Young trees supported by the roots of a parent tree have a better chance of survival than a single seedling. A tightly packed grove provides better protection from too much sun, too. I have survived forest fires that burnt neighboring forests to the ground, because my roots will keep on producing new suckers.

My type of tree is the most widely spread tree species in North America. Our groves stretch the entire width of Canada and scientists estimate that we cover tens of millions of acres in North America.

God thought of everything when he created me —**Giant Quaking Aspen.**

More on the Web

Learn more about this amazing giant aspen grove at:

http://www.extremescience.com/aspengrove.htm

Tell a Friend

Do you "quake" at the slightest problem in your life? Remember this: When we invite Jesus into our hearts and lives, we are "rooted" in him. He supplies all we need to grow. He will increase our faith as we depend on him day by day.

Read About It

"Have your roots in him. Build yourselves up in him. Grow strong in what you believe, just as you were taught. Be more thankful than ever before." —Colossians 2:7

Did you know, the Bible compares kind words to a tree? Read about it in Proverbs 15:4.

Pray About It

Lord, thank you for helping me grow into the person you want me to be!

HOME SWEET SOCK DRAWER

During late fall, you might notice me hanging in a cluster on the side of your house or shed. My family and I are looking for openings around windows, doors, and foundations. Winter is coming, and we want in! Who needs scratchy bushes and trees when a warm, soft drawer full of socks is available? Who needs blustery winter winds, when there is a warm attic or wall to call home?

Once settled cozily inside, I'm not a demanding houseguest. In fact, I won't move or eat until late winter or early spring. You might not even notice me until my huge family and I start waking up in the spring. Then watch out! Our main goal is to find our way back outside.

Although I'm a harmless pest indoors, farmers and gardeners appreciate my help. God gave me a huge appetite for aphids—tiny insects that damage certain trees, roses, and crops. If the aphid population is too big for me to handle, I send out a special message by releasing a special chemical scent. The scent attracts others in my family, and we plan a big aphid potluck.

God thought of everything when he created me—**Asian Lady Beetle.**

More on the Web

Four Asian lady beetles traveled with their favorite food—aphids—into space in 1999. Find out what scientists learned about their behavior on a gravity-free space shuttle.

http://www.zoomschool.com/subjects/insects/ladybug/Ladybug.shtml/

Tell a Friend

The Asian lady beetle serves a good purpose—to help control harmful insects that damage crops and trees. God has a special purpose in mind for your life, too. Have you asked him to reveal it to you?

Read About It

"I will always guide you. I will satisfy your needs in a land that is baked by the sun. I will make you stronger. You will be like a garden that has plenty of water. You will be like a spring that never runs dry."

—Isaiah 58:11

I am the only lady beetle with a marking on my body that looks like the upside-down letter M.

Pray About It

Dear God, thank you for creating me with a special purpose in mind! Please guide me to the plan you have for my life.

AN ANT'S WORST NIGHTMARE

Move over, anteaters! I am a lizard with an appetite for ants, especially small black ants. Scientists estimate that I can eat anywhere from 600 to 3,000 ants in a single meal. I flick them one by one onto my sticky tongue.

When I am not gorging myself on ants, I work hard at keeping cool in my home on Australia's desert. I dig a shallow, underground burrow beneath small shrubs. I don't worry about predators, either, because God taught me how to protect myself perfectly: I change color to match the sandy soil. If an enemy finds my hiding place, I tuck my head between my front legs, leaving a knob-like bump that looks like a fake head.

Try to flip me over, and I'll press my spiny covering into the ground and refuse to budge. If that doesn't scare off a predator, I can always puff myself up to appear larger. Are you scared yet?

God provides water exactly when I need it. My back is covered with thorns and tiny grooves in a pattern that resembles a system of canals. The grooves trap heavy dew or rain. When I need a drink of water, I gulp. That movement moves water along the grooves, to the corner of my mouth where I can drink as much as I need.

God thought of everything when he created me—**Thorny Devil.**

More on the Web

In 1841, a scientist named John Gray gave me the scientific name *moloch horridus.* Read details about those early studies:

http://uts.cc.utexas.edu/~varanus/moloch.html

Tell a Friend

Think of a time when you were so thirsty, you could hardly wait to reach a water faucet. God promises us another kind of water—living water. Read the verse below and talk about what living water means to you.

Read About It

"Does anyone believe in me? Then, just as Scripture says, streams of living water will flow from inside him."—John 7:38

I lay eggs in an air-filled chamber underground. When the eggs hatch, my young eat the shells as a valuable source of calcium.

Pray About It

Heavenly Father, thank you for sending Jesus to quench my spiritual thirst!

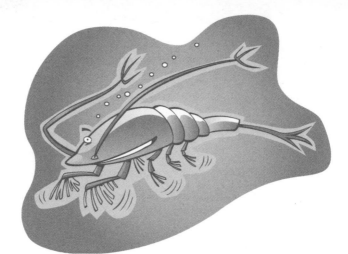

FROM ESCAPE ARTIST TO PARASITE

I'm a small shrimp-like creature without a backbone, called a *crustacean*. Some of my cousins live in lakes and ponds, but I live in the ocean.

God created me with many legs for swimming and gathering food. I feast on one-celled goodies like bacteria and diatom. With a pumping motion, I suck the creatures toward my jaws, called *mandibles*, which process the food. And like a picky toddler, I sometimes spit out food I don't like.

Two sets of antennae keep me from sinking. They are also my built-in alarm system. Covered with tiny sensors, they let me know how fast the surrounding water is moving, and alert me whenever there's sudden movement in the water. One simple eye in the middle of my head detects changes in light. God gave me lightning-fast reflexes that help me avoid danger. I'm a regular escape artist!

When I grow up, I will attach myself to a fish for life (I'm partial to Atlantic cod). I will no longer dart about, but draw nourishment from the flesh and blood of my host. As a female, I will spend the rest of my life producing eggs from my new home on the fin of a fish.

God thought of everything when he created me—**Copepod.**

More on the Web

Here's a printable, detailed illustration of a copepod.

http://www.enchantedlearning.com/paint/subjects/invertebrates/crustacean/Copepod.shtml

Tell a Friend

Just like the copepod, God wants to help *us* avoid harmful things, too. He wants us to seek his guidance when we're faced with big decisions or tempted by sin.

Read About It

"I will guide you and teach you the way you should go. I will give you good advice and watch over you." —Psalm 32:8

Pray About It

Lord, thank you for giving me guidance and wisdom. You take such good care of me! Remind me that you are just a prayer away.

Like a snake, I shed my skin 11 times during my development. At each shedding, I grow a little bigger.

SCRATCHING OUT A LIVING

I was born in a gigantic nest called a mound. On the second day of life, I began foraging for food and drinking water all by myself. I did not have a mother or father to nudge me along. God taught me everything I know.

I am now a big-footed male bird with a mighty responsibility. To attract a mate, I must first prepare a mound, 15 feet across and four feet high. Using my claws, I rake leaves and other forest matter into a circle. From twilight to dawn, I work for days until my nest is finished.

Once satisfied, I hollow out holes where eggs will incubate. The nest must maintain a certain temperature or eggs will die, so God gave me a tongue that works like a thermometer! If I discover a cold section, I pile more leaves there—like adding another blanket to a bed. If I notice a hot spot, I open air holes.

After mating, a female lays one egg per hole, then runs away. That is when my real work begins! I monitor the nest's temperature for about two months. I also guard it from egg-loving predators like the carpet snake. Soon after hatching, baby scrub turkeys begin life on their own. My job is now complete—until it's time for me to build another nest, that is.

God thought of everything when he created me—**Australian Scrub Turkey.**

More on the Web

Want to hear an Australian scrub turkey?

http://lamington.nrsm.uq.edu.au/docs/Birds/Scrub.htm

Tell a Friend

The Australian scrub turkey sticks to its job until it is completed. God gives us opportunities to show that we are responsible, too. In everything we do, we should work as if we are completing a job for him.

Read About It

"My dear brothers and sisters, stand firm. Don't let anything move you. Always give yourselves completely to the work of the Lord. Because you belong to the Lord, you know that your work is not worthless."—1 Corinthians 15:58

My hatchlings receive no parenting. Once they hatch, they are on their own.

Pray About It

Lord, help me to stick to the job you have given me to complete—even when it's tough or boring.

KNOCK KNOCK!
ANYONE OUT THERE?

I develop inside a warm, cozy egg for about two months. My shell was not very big, and there came a time when I needed fresh air. God planned a way for me to break out of my hard shell. He created a special tool that I could use for slicing through the soft inner layer. However, that's not all; He knew I'd need something extra-hard to crack open the rock-hard outer layer of shell, too.

His solution was an *egg tooth*—a tough chunk of skin that sits on top of my snout. Formed long before I was ready to leave the security of my egg, the egg tooth was ready whenever I needed it. When the big moment arrived, I used it as my ticket to freedom.

First, I rubbed the tip of my snout up and down inside the egg. Then I whacked the shell a few times, to split open the hard outer layer. I used my egg tooth only once. After bursting out of my shell into the fresh air, I no longer had a use for it. Several weeks after I hatched it disappeared back into my body, never to be seen again. It had served its purpose, by doing the important job God planned for it to do.

God thought of everything when he created me—**Crocodile.**

More on the Web

Learn what it's like to be a crocodile:

http://www.kingsnake.com/oz/crocs/porosus.htm

Tell a Friend

Our Creator oversees the birth of a crocodile by giving it a way to crack its own egg. The Bible tells us that God watches a baby as he or she develops inside its mother, too. He orchestrates every detail of those early months, and longs for us to trust him for the rest of our lives, too.

Read About It

"None of my bones was hidden from you when you made me inside my mother's body."—Psalm 139:15

Certain adult saltwater crocodiles have been known to swim for over 600 miles between islands or around coastlines.

Pray About It

Thank you for the gift of life, dear God. Help me to use it in a way that brings honor to you.

MY LIFE'S A MASQUERADE PARTY

C ertain *entomologists* (people who study insects) think I'm related
to the lowly cockroach. *Harrumph!* If you ask me, my species is
much more creative than a cockroach. We are masters of disguise.
Some of my relatives have fancy bodies like flowers. They look so
convincing, insects land on them in search of sweet nectar! Others
have the God-given ability to change their coloring to blend in with
their surroundings.

I look like a crinkly, brown leaf. Most people and predators pass
right by without realizing I am an insect. I use my disguise as a protection against my enemies, as well as a way to sneak up on my next meal.

I have over 2,000 cousins. I've heard rumors that some of my
family members are kept as pets, but in Malaysia, we can grow six to
ten inches long! Would you want an insect that size lumbering around
your bedroom?

God designed my body with an extra-long neck. It enables me to move my head back and forth 180 degrees. I have two large eyes on the sides of my triangle-shaped head, for viewing images and color. Three smaller eyes sit in a triangle shape between my antennae, and help me detect darkness from light.

When hungry, I react quickly. My claw-like legs dart out, hook an unsuspecting cricket or lizard, and CRUNCH—he's history! If I'm extra hungry, I can grab and hold one critter while munching on another. You could say I'm an excellent multi-tasker.

God thought of everything when he created me—**Dead-Leaf Mantid.**

More on the Web

Here's my family album. That's cousin Flora in the orchid costume.
http://www.bugsincyberspace.com/mantids/

Tell a Friend

The dead-leaf mantid is a master of disguise. Sometimes people try to disguise their true feelings from others, but nobody can fool God. He invites us to relax and just be ourselves.

Read About It

"But God is greater than our hearts. He knows everything."
—1 John 3:20

My eyes are sensitive to the slightest movement up to 60 feet away!

Pray About It

Lord, thank you for loving me the way I am. Help me to love myself as you do, so I can be the person you created me to be.

SALTSHAKER OF THE SHORELINE

I was planted on the Mediterranean shoreline as a windbreaker—a tree that slows the force of strong winds blowing in off the sea. I am able to tolerate the harsh, dry climate and salty soil of this region. If I were to catch fire or were chopped down, I would send up new shoots and start again.

Tourists sometimes wonder if I have died, because my small, feathery leaves give me a wilted appearance. But inside my bushy branches is a survivor. I can live in soil that has hardly any nutrients. I don't require fresh water, and here on the shores of Crete, I soak up to 1,100 liters of *salt water* every day. Talk about thirsty!

God showed me how to expel excess salt from seawater. It collects on the tips of my leaves like powder, and discourages insects from munching on me. Thanks to salt, I am free of parasites and disease.

I grow a foot per month every spring, and will produce up to 500,000 windblown seeds. New trees have sprung up all around the world. Some were even discovered growing high in the nearby mountains, at an elevation of 7,000 feet!

God thought of everything when he created me—**Tamarisk Tree.**

More on the Web

The tamarisk doesn't look like a typical tree, does it?

http://members.tripod.com/~bbowles/tamarisk.html

Tell a Friend

Strong winds and a blazing sun cannot destroy the tamarisk. In much the same way, God helps us to stand against problems that blow into our life. With his help, we can weather anything.

Read About It

"But I will bless any man who trusts in me. I will show my favor to the one who depends on me. He will be like a tree that is planted near water. It sends out its roots beside a stream. It is not afraid when heat comes. Its leaves are always green. It does not worry when there is no rain. It always bears fruit."
—Jeremiah 17:7, 8

The Bible says that Abraham planted one of my ancestors in Beersheba. Read about it in Genesis 21:33

Pray About It

Lord, help me to understand your Word, so that I can stand strong when problems blow into my life.

BRING ON THE BEES!

I roost in a small colony of brightly colored birds like myself. We live high in the treetops along coastal areas of Africa, the Middle East, and from Russia to Asia. I am a stunning shade of green, with—you guessed it—blue cheeks!

Don't expect to find me pecking for worms like a robin on a damp lawn. I thrive on a steady diet of *stinging* insects like hornets, wasps, ants, and bees! Other birds would not dare try to catch a bee, but what's the big deal?

I perch on a high wire or tree branch until I spot my prey. If a bee lands near me on a branch, I ignore it. God gave me instructions to catch insects only during flight. Catching them off guard is the key to a successful hunt. I swoop down and snap up my clueless victims before they know what hit them.

God custom-designed my bill for chasing down bees. My long, narrow bill is positioned a safe distance from my eyes, so an angry bee can't deliver a blinding sting. Once I catch a bee, I whack it several times against a tree branch, or give it a big, strong squeeze to rid it of venom. Then it's lunch time.

If I can't find enough stinging insects for one day, I'll settle for dragonflies, butterflies, and grasshoppers. But nothing quite hits the spot like a meal of crunchy hornets, topped off with a wasp for dessert.

God thought of everything when he created me—**Blue-Cheeked Bee-Eater.**

More on the Web
See why I'm called a blue-cheeked bee-eater?

http://www.montereybay.com/creagrus/bee-eaters.html

Tell a Friend
God has taught bee-eating birds how to avoid a painful and poisonous sting. Did you know words can sting, too? When someone says something hurtful, how do you react?

Read About It
"Lord, may the words of my mouth and the thoughts of my heart be pleasing in your eyes. You are my Rock and my Redeemer."
—Psalm 19:14

Because I thrive in sunny climates, you won't find me anywhere in Britain.

Pray About It
Lord, I can't control how others treat me, but I can control my reaction to their words. Help me to turn to you instead of trying to get even.

PINK PARENTS OF THE LAGOON

I'm four feet tall, but only weigh 16 pounds. That's less than some Thanksgiving turkeys! My long, skinny legs are perfect for sifting through mud in the soggy coastal lagoons of South America. God gave me an oversized, curved bill, but no teeth. I have a large tongue, which forces water and mud through a sort of filter. The filter collects food like worms, insect larvae, and tiny plants like algae and diatoms.

My webbed feet have four toes—three in front and the fourth high at the back. These feet would not work for an animal that needs to climb, but my Creator knew I would need to steady myself in the slippery lagoon. My feet grip mud like suction cups.

For the sake of safety, my mate and I live in a colony of several thousand birds. The two of us built a nest out of mud and vegetation. Our nest is six to twelve inches high, with a 12-inch hollow area in the top. When I breed in the spring, I lay a single oblong-shaped egg in that spot.

Both of us take turns sitting on the egg for 28 to 31 days each. After welcoming our grayish white chick into the world, we take turns feeding it, too. Our baby will not be able to fend for itself until it is about two months old, but together we prepare it for independence.

God thought of everything when he created me—**Flamingo.**

More on the Web

Compare different types of flamingoes in this photo collection online.

http://www.natureportfolio.com/birds/flamingos.php

Tell a Friend

God equipped the flamingo with feet that would help steady it from falling. The Bible also keeps us from falling by increasing our faith and strengthening our commitment to Jesus.

Some of the food in my diet contains high amounts of a special pigment called carotene. If I eat a lot of it, it will turn my new feathers pink and red.

Read About It

"The Lord is faithful and will keep all of his promises. He is loving toward everything he has made."
—Psalm 145:13

Pray About It

Thank you for being a trustworthy Savior and Lord. Help me to know you better through your Word.

TIC-TAC-TOE . . . WATCH MY WEB GROW!

At first glance, my web looks like a normal spider web, but step closer. See those thick zigzag lines in the shape of a large X? Researchers have tested them, and discovered that they are made from a different kind of silk than I use for the rest of my web. Those strands reflect ultraviolet light, which tricks flying insects into thinking my web is a fancy flower.

I cling to the zigzag X and wait there with my eight legs separated in pairs. From a distance, I look like a dangling game of tic-tac-toe. My feet have three claws each—one more than most spiders.

When an insect flies into my web, I wrap its body in strands of silk until it can no longer move. Then I ring a dinner bell. *Yummy*!

If a hungry predator tries to catch me, I have an emergency plan. God taught me to vibrate my web so the outline of my body is blurred.

If that does not confuse my visitor, I can flip through an escape hatch to the other side of the web, then drop to the ground. I can also wiggle my abdomen to expose a pair of large black dots—scary, fake eyes. That usually does the trick!

God thought of everything when he created me—**St. Andrew's Cross Spider.**

More on the Web

Enjoy colorful photos of the St. Andrew's cross spider.

http://www.rochedalss.qld.edu.au/stand.htm

Tell a Friend

God taught the spider a way of escape. It instinctively knows how to run from danger. Jesus provides a way of escape for us, too. With his help, we can run from temptation.

Read About It

"When you are tempted, God will give you a way out so that you can stand up under it."
—1 Corinthians 10:13

The Bible teaches that anyone who forgets God is like a person who leans on a spider's web. Find out more by reading Job 8: 13-15.

Pray About It

Lord, when I run into a sticky web of temptation, help me to remember that it's never too late to turn away. Thank you for giving me an escape hatch where I can seek help from you.

I GET CARRIED AWAY

I was named for J.F. Wolff, an 18th century German physician and *botanist* (a person who studies plants). I am the world's smallest flowering plant, and a member of the duckweed family.

God created me without roots, so I don't require soil. I simply float on the surface of a body of water, such as a pond or a quiet stream. Part of me is visible from above as a delicate flower, and the rest lives underwater. If you were to rub me between your fingers or hands, I would feel like fine grain or meal. That is why I am sometimes referred to as "watermeal." I look like fine green grains floating in the water.

When my fruit bursts, my seed sinks to the bottom of the pond, but that's not the end. God planned an awesome voyage for my tiny blossom. Water birds such as ducks land in the pond, and seeds stick to their feet. Because birds tuck their feet close to their bodies in flight, it's easy for seeds to hitch a ride from pond to pond! In the southeastern United States there are records of whole plant bodies being carried by a tornado, or frozen inside hailstones!

God thought of everything when he created me—**Wolffia.**

More on the Web

Wolffia is the smallest type of duckweed plant. Check it out!

http://www.mobot.org/jwcross/duckweed/duckpix.htm

Tell a Friend

Even the tiniest flowering plant in the world can spread and grow, thanks to God's plan. As believers in Christ, we play an important role in spreading his love. Are you treating others in a way that helps them to see Jesus' love?

Read About It

"Dear children, don't just talk about love. Put your love into action. Then it will truly be love."—1 John 3:18

I measure less than 1/25 of an inch! My fruit is smaller than a grain of table salt! It is even smaller than a single cell of many plants and animals.

Pray About It

Lord, thank you for loving me so much. I want others to know your love, too. Help me to pass your love on to my friends and family who don't know you.

A DEADLY SURPRISE

I grew from a long strand of about 30,000 eggs, laid in a small pond by my mother. A male toad fertilized the eggs, and within three days we had hatched. I looked like a typical jet-black tadpole—tiny, wiggly, and cute. My shape changed quickly, though, and I turned into a toadlet and hopped away one day.

I'm now a hefty, warty amphibian from Australia—a toad that looks and behaves much differently than other toads. You'll recognize me by the bony ridge above each eye, and the oversized glands on both my shoulders. God planned those glands so I would have a way to protect myself. They produce poison, called *venom*, which I am able to ooze if an enemy bothers me. I have smaller poison storage glands spread over my entire warty body.

When a predator comes too close, I flip over on my side and point my shoulder glands at it. An animal receiving a dose of my poison will die within 15 minutes! If a sneaky intruder tries to eat me, he'll be in for a deadly surprise, too. I'm a poisonous snack even as a tiny toadlet. Humans can't escape my wrath, either. Those who try to trap me quickly discover that my venom can cause intense pain and temporary blindness.

God thought of everything when he created me—**Cane Toad.**

More on the Web

Learn why Australia imported 150 cane toads back in 1935.

http://www.jcu.edu.au/school/phtm/PHTM/staff/rsbufo.htm

Tell a Friend

God provides animals like the cane toad with a way to protect themselves from predators who would harm them. God gives believers his Word as a strong shield. Which verses have helped you in times of trouble?

Read About It

"God's way is perfect. The word of the Lord doesn't have any flaws. He is like a shield to all who go to him for safety."—Psalm 18:30

A few native animals of Australia have learned how to snack on only my non-toxic parts.

Pray About It

Thank you for sending your Word to protect me. Teach me to depend on it daily.

FLASHLIGHT OF THE AMAZON

I'm a rare insect with a lot of nicknames. My family originated in China, but I live near the Amazon River in South America. I was born with a long forehead, and a large, snout-like growth on my head. Curving upward, my snout's bumpy design looks like a peanut shell. My odd-shaped head is hollow and leads down into my digestive tract. The main attraction, though, happens every now and then, when my head lights up like a flashlight!

Natives in this region are afraid of my light. They believe that a bite from me means sure death. That's not true, though, because I don't bite! I have a special mouthpiece like a drinking straw, which I use to suck nutrients from plants.

God gave me a creative way to protect myself: I pretend I'm a lizard, like the lizards that scurry along the branches of my favorite feeding trees. I also try to scare intruders by opening my wings and flashing two bright red and black spots at them. The spots look like huge eyes. If that doesn't work, I give up and spray them with a chemical. My body manufactures the spray as the result of eating toxic tree resins. The resin doesn't make me sick, but the resulting toxic spray will stop an enemy dead in its tracks.

God thought of everything when he created me—**Lanternfly.**

More on the Web

Here's a photo taken in my natural habitat:

http://entweb.clemson.edu/museum/misc/misc/misc11.htm

Tell a Friend

The lanternfly uses caution when meeting other creatures of the rainforest. It imitates a lizard! The Bible tells us we should imitate Jesus. He loves us, and will never lead us in a wrong direction.

Read About It

"You are the children that God dearly loves. So be just like him. Lead a life of love, just as Christ did."
—Ephesians 5:1, 2

Pray About It

Thank you for setting an example that I can follow, Lord. Give me courage to stand up for what I believe.

Natives of the Amazon rainforest call me also call me "alligator bug"

A BLOSSOMING FRIENDSHIP

The yucca is an amazing flowering plant, divided into about 40 different types. It is known for the amazing way it pollinates. *Ta-da!* That's where I come in. I'm a moth with the God-given ability to stuff a tiny ball of pollen into the cup-shaped center of each flower. The yucca plant needs me so much, if I don't show up it stops producing seeds. Imagine that—a plant who waits for a certain moth to arrive for duty!

Moths like me can be found in the southwestern United States and Mexico, plus certain areas of the Caribbean Islands. Each spring, male and female members of my species slither out of our cocoons and fly to nearby yucca plants.

I lay my eggs in a yucca flower, and deposit a rolled ball of pollen into the stigma of the plant. As pollen grains germinate, they send hundreds of fertilized seeds deep into the flower's ovary. When my larva hatches during late spring and early summer, it awakes in a "room" surrounded by flowers and delicious food.

By early autumn, the larva emerges from its feeding room and drops to the ground. There it burrows into the rain-softened soil and builds a silky cocoon. It stays inside its cocoon during the long rainy months of winter. When temperatures finally warm up, an adult moth emerges and begins its search for—what else?—a flowering yucca plant.

God thought of everything when he created me—**Yucca Moth.**

More on the Web

Close-up photos show details of the yucca moth in action:

http://waynesword.palomar.edu/ww0902c.htm

Tell a Friend

The yucca tree and moth have a partnership that works perfectly. A good friendship follows that same pattern of give and take. How do you and your best friend give to one another?

The Bible compares an evil person's house to a moth's cocoon. Read about it in Job 27:18.

Read About It

"Love each other deeply. Honor others more than yourselves."—Romans 12:10

Pray About It

Thanks for being a good friend, Lord, and for setting an example for me to follow.

PARTNERS FOR LIFE

If you searched all day, you still wouldn't find me. I am a bacteria that's visible only through the lens of a microscope. Some bacteria are harmful, but God gave me a specific job to do. I carry out my duties by living in soil and inside plants.

First, I attach myself to the root hairs of a plant. That's when the fun begins! Once I set up housekeeping, I release a substance that causes them to curl. A team of us forms a line and spreads deep inside those roots. Like an army, we split into groups and go to work. We invade bumpy growths on the plant's stem called *nodules*.

I considered a nitrogen-fixing bacteria, because green plants need me. They are unable to use natural nitrogen directly from the air, but thanks to God, I know the formula for changing natural nitrogen into a simpler substance called *nitrates*. Green plants need nitrates to live. See why I love my job?

I help the plant, and the plant, in turn, helps me. Cells within those bumpy nodules supply oxygen for me to breathe. The plant also provides a safe home and a steady supply of carbon, which gives me energy. The carbon is produced from light—sunshine! My army of bacteria and I work together in a friendly partnership to help our host plant grow tall and strong.

God thought of everything when he created me—**Rizobium.**

More on the Web

Want to see what a nodule looks like? Here is a photo of a soybean plant covered with them. Inside each bump lives thousands of bacteria just like me.

http://www.agnet.org/library/image/ac1994e1.html

Tell a Friend

God taught microscopic bacteria and plants to work together as partners and he teaches men, women, boys, and girls how to live in harmony, too. Are you helping or hurting your friendships?

Read About It

"A friend loves at all times. He is there to help when trouble comes." —Proverbs 17:17

Pray About It

Please forgive me for the times when I act uncooperative, Lord. Show me how to give of myself, as Jesus did.

Cows can thank me for the nitrogen in the grass they eat.

SOMETHING'S FISHY!

My mother laid her eggs in a jelly-like substance. Her eggs floated on the surface of the sea in sheets until they were ready to hatch. I hatched as a female. I am a most unusual fish, with a special growth hanging from my forehead. It lights up to guide me through the murky waters along the sea bottom, where I forage for food. When it's time to mate, the soft glow of my light also attracts a male of my species.

After mating, we stick together for life—literally. The male grips my skin with sharp, pincer-like teeth (*ouch!*), and from that day on, I tow him through the water like a trailer. To attract my next meal, I wiggle a "flashlight" lure from a long appendage on my forehead.

Over the next few weeks, strange things happen to his body. His skin become spiny and fuses with mine at his jaw area. His eyes grow smaller and finally dissolve. Only two holes remain open, one on each side of his mouth. Those allow him to draw in water for breathing.

It's a good thing God gave me a stretchy stomach, so I could eat for two. My mate eventually receives food directly from my bloodstream, which now begins circulating through his body, too. Now, how weird is *that*?

God thought of everything when he created me—**Angler Fish.**

More on the Web

Here's a page of angler fish facts, and a detailed photo from the Monterey Bay Aquarium:

http://www.mbayaq.org/efc/living_species/default.asp?hOri=1&inhab=176

Tell a Friend

God takes delight in his creation. He didn't bring us into the world and then forget about us, but lovingly provided a guidebook—his Word—as a "flashlight" to light our way! How well do you know your Bible? Memorize a verse every week with a friend, and by the end of one year, you'll each know 52 new Bible verses to light your way.

Read About It

"Your word is like a lamp that shows me the way. It is like a light that guides me."—Psalm 119:105

The Bible contains a lot of very fishy stories! Read Matthew 14:14-20 to see how Jesus used two small fish.

Pray About It

Thanks, Lord, for giving me your special guidebook, the Bible, to show me how to live.

A PRICKLY HITCHHIKER

I ride from place to place by hooking onto socks, shoes, or other clothing. If livestock or a pet brushes against me, I'll cling so tightly, it takes scissors to remove me. My burs contain air spaces that allow me to float for up to 30 days, too, so if I fall into a stream it's not a problem.

I grow on a plant in the middle of a wet, weedy field. My plant needs 15 full hours of darkness. Darkness helps release a protein pigment that tells me when to produce flowers! A single burst of light is enough to stop this process, so my plant never blooms during summer.

I may be a lowly weed, but God used my sticky burs to spark a good idea. In 1948, a Swiss mountaineer, George de Mestral, went on a nature walk with his dog. When they returned home, Mestral's dog was covered with burs. Mestral was curious and inspected the burs under a microscope, to see how they managed to cling so tightly to his clothes and to his dog's fur.

He noticed a hook-and-loop design, which led him to create a two-sided fastener that we know as Velcro. Velcro is used in backpacks, shoes, and by NASA, to keep equipment from floating around in the weightless environment of space.

God thought of everything when he created me—**Cocklebur.**

More on the Web

Weeds come in all sizes, shapes, and colors. Compare cocklebur to other weeds in this colorful collection of photos from Rutgers University:

http://www.rce.rutgers.edu/weeds/index-thumbnail.asp

Tell a Friend

God uses even those sticky, hitchhiking cockleburs. Have you considered how he can use your talents and abilities, too? Why not ask him where he'd like you to begin?

Read About It

"God's gifts of grace come in many forms. Each of you has received a gift in order to serve others. You should use it faithfully."—1 Peter 4:10

Pray About It

Heavenly Father, sometimes I feel as useless as a wild weed. Please show me ways I can make a difference in my world.

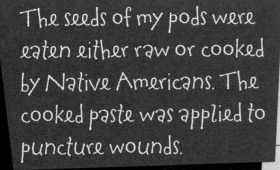

The seeds of my pods were eaten either raw or cooked by Native Americans. The cooked paste was applied to puncture wounds.

ACROBAT OF THE AIR

I f not for me, you'd have to put up with more flies and mosquito bites. I'm a glutton for mosquitoes, flies, and gnats, and my appetite helps control the number of those pesky critters.

Catching my dinner is no small task, but God equipped me with excellent vision. Each of my eyes are made up of thousands of individual lenses, called *facets*, and are so big, they meet at the top of my head. I look like a set of flying eyeballs! I am able to detect even the slightest movement, so there's no use trying to catch me. I can spot you sneaking up on me from 40 feet away.

God designed four amazing wings for me. Delicately veined and transparent, they're not only pretty; they turn me into an agile acrobat. I'm among the fastest winged insects alive. My wings work together to help me accurately stop, start, and shift directions suddenly. Each set of wings works independently, too. I can flap them together, or one set at a time. It's not unusual to see my back wings flapping down while my front wings are lifting up.

Certain members of my family have been clocked at 36 miles per hour. My wingspan is about five inches wide, but scientists found a fossil of one of my ancestors with a wingspan of almost 30 inches! The smallest of my species is from Borneo, with a wingspan of less than an inch.

God thought of everything when he created me—**Dragonfly.**

More on the Web

This is the closest you will ever get to a dragonfly, thanks to insect photographer Steve Hoffman:

http://www.ivyhall.district96.k12.il.us/4th/kkhp/1insects/dragclose.html

Tell a Friend

Dragonfly's wings work together, and so can friends! Think of a time when you cooperated with a friend to accomplish a special project. How did it feel to see the end result?

Read About It

"Don't be proud at all. Be completely gentle. Be patient. Put up with one another in love."—Ephesians 4:2

Pray About It

Give me a heart that is willing to cooperate with others, Lord.

It is rare for members of my species to survive a whole year.

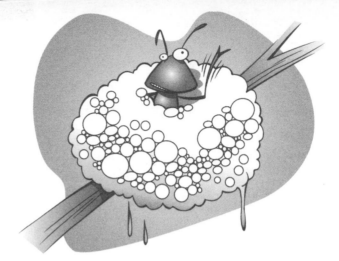

PROTECTED BY A FOAMY FORT

A couple of months ago, my mother laid eggs on a leafy green plant. She chose a spot where her babies would grow safely. Inside my egg, I went through five stages designed by God.

God kept me warm and safe while I was a baby, called a *nymph*. He showed me how to produce bubbly foam mixed with air. I used the goo to build myself a fort for protection, by wrapping it around the stem of a plant. When my gob of spit reached the size of a large grape, I crawled inside. Inside my frothy fort, I was safe from predators on the prowl for a tasty snack.

My spittle fort kept me warm in cold weather and cool on hot summer afternoons. Moisture from the spittle also kept my body from drying out. Who but God could have thought of such a plan?

I didn't have a spine or wings in those early days, and as I grew, I changed colors. I changed from yellow to green to brown. I'm now dark brownish black with bright orange stripes. My head is shaped like a frog's head, with dark eyes arranged at the sides. I have wings, but am also skilled at jumping, thanks to strong, springy hind legs.

God thought of everything when he created me—**Spittlebug.**

More on the Web

Want to see what spittlebugs look like in every stage of growth? Read what one gardener from Maine thinks of this pesky garden invader.

http://www.hillgardens.com/spittlebugs.htm

Tell a Friend

God created everything with an eye for detail. When's the last time you thanked him for taking such good care of you? He provides shelter, warmth, food, and so much more!

Read About It

"How good it is to sing praises to our God! How pleasant and right it is to praise him!"—Psalm 147:1

Pray About It

Lord, you provide exactly what I need for each day. Thank you!

It takes 45 to 52 days for me to turn into a winged adult.

LOOK, MA! NO CAVITIES!

I'm about one third the size of a football field, with gill slits that wrap almost around my head. My most recognizable feature, though, is my huge mouth. I am a slow swimmer, creeping along at only three miles per hour.

I live by the buddy system, traveling in groups as small as three or four, up to large schools of 100. *Relax!* We're harmless to humans. We travel the balmy waters off the coasts of both North and South America.

God thought of an awesome system for filtering water. I swim with my mouth wide open! Water flows into my mouth, along with plankton, fish eggs, and different varieties of baby fish. When I close my mouth, special spiky growths called *gill rakers* go to work. Like a sieve, they sort out only the food I want to eat.

I won't settle for breakfasting on cod or snacking on snapper—no sir! Instead, I prefer plankton—tiny plants and animals that float along near the water's surface. Plankton supplies the energy I need to make my way through the water. If I find myself swimming in an area lacking in plankton, I'll lose strength quickly, and won't have enough energy to hold my mouth open while I swim.

God thought of everything when he created me—**Basking Shark.**

More on the Web

See how my unusual gill rakers work!

http://www.austmus.gov.au/fishes/fishfacts/fish/cmaximus2.htm

Tell a Friend

The basking shark isn't used to swimming all alone. Humans were not created to travel through life by ourselves, either. We need each other, but even more: God knew that we would need a Savior, and sent Jesus. What does Jesus mean to you?

Read About It

"God's grace has saved you because of your faith in Christ. Your salvation doesn't come from anything you do. It is God's gift. It is not based on anything you have done. No one can brag about earning it."—Ephesians 2:8,9

Pray About It

Dear God, thank you for providing what I need most—a Savior! Help me to travel side-by-side with Jesus all the days of my life.

I am the next-to-largest fish in the sea, weighing in at over seven tons!

SURVIVING
MIDDLE SCHOOL
written by
Sandy Silverthorne
0-7847-1433-9

BELIEVE IT!
written by
Steven James
0-7847-1393-6

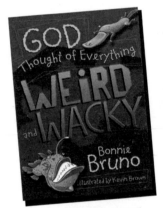

GOD THOUGHT OF
EVERYTHING
WEIRD AND WACKY
written by
Bonnie Bruno
0-7847-1447-9

GOD THOUGHT OF
EVERYTHING
STRANGE AND SLIMY
written by
Bonnie Bruno
0-7847-1448-7